EMPOWER YOURSELF
Self Development
for Women

Eve Warren and Caroline Gielnik

THE INDUSTRIAL SOCIETY

First published in 1995 by
The Industrial Society
Robert Hyde House
48 Bryanston Square
London W1H 7LN
Telephone: 071–262 2401

© The Industrial Society 1995

ISBN 1 85835 244 4

British Library Cataloguing-in-Publication Data.
A catalogue record for this book is available from the
British Library

Typeset by: Photoprint, Torquay
Printed by: Alden Press
Cover design: Nicky Downes

Text illustrations (cartoons): Rachel Busch

The Industrial Society is a Registered Charity No. 29003

ACKNOWLEDGEMENTS

We would like to express our thanks for the support and inspiration we have received from the people who have so generously shared their experience, expertise and skills to make this book possible.

Patricia Adams, Linda Amili, Debra Alcock, Liz Armah, Sonia Arnold, Helen Arnott, Chloe Asprey, Maura Bagnall, Caroline Barnett, Cheryl Bell, Barbara Brown, Julie Byrne, Ivy Cameron, Diana Clarke, Sue Coryndon, Debbie Cottam, Cheryl Davis, Terry Denny, Mariella Dexter, Jo Emery, Florence Fernadez, Joanne Gardiner, Christine Garner, Angela Gielnik, Pat Ghosh, Vanda Green, Tamara Grigulis, Barbara Hamilton, Judy Hardogan, Anne Haverda, Lisa Hooper, Marion Ives, Inike Jansen, Cassandra Jefferies, Kate Keefe, Jennifer King, Claire Laing, Heather Lang, Vanessa Lidsay, Colleen McCabe, Rowena McConnochie, Samantha Mabb, Linda MacLaughlan, Marjory Mair, Alison Mead, Jane Meyler, Stephanie Mills, Claire Mullins, Niamah Murtag, Parul Patel, Liz Paton, Kay Phelan, Naomi Phillips, Anne Pickman, Jan Quinlan, Suzanne Robinson-Hyde, Amanda Rogers, Joanna Rose, Rosie Smith, Sue Spencer, Nicola Talman, Caroline

Toll, Paula Verlinden, Anne Vickers, Nicola Whitmarsh.

Unable to individually acknowledge everyone else who has inspired this work, we nonetheless include the women who have shared their stories over the years in our appreciation. Particularly we are grateful to the 100 women who responded to our questionnaire and those who have contributed through their participation on our courses. Finally, we also thank Dennis Merrigan and Sheridan Maguire for their patience and encouragement.

ELIZABETH PEPPERELL

We acknowledge our debt to Elizabeth Pepperell. In 1952, when assistant Director of the Industrial Society, she held the first single sex conference for women. With her vision of a better future she campaigned to raise awareness of the training and career issues for women and encouraged women's access to training and development opportunities. She laid the foundations for the practical courses that have evolved over the years, focusing on the specific concerns of working women. The Society's work that bears her name reaches thousands of women each year.

Introduction   xiii

PART I: EMPOWERMENT – BEGINNING THE PROCESS   1

1   Taking responsibility   3
What is the challenge?   3
    Women's career experience   6
What disempowers us?   10
    The influence of stereotypes   10
    Gender and career planning   13
    Costs and benefits   15
What stops us taking responsibility?   16
    Do I have a choice?   16
    Thinking negatively about the future   17
    Focusing on the past   18
    Being too busy in the present   20
    The effect it would have on others   21
Links with self-esteem   24
Deciding to change   26
    The Pepperell Box   26
    What does success mean to me?   28
    Role models   31
Summary – Practical tips   32

2   Eyes on the hills – feet on the ground   33
Career and life planning   33
    Life as a process of change   35
    Taking time   37
Career development framework   39
    Looking back   40
    Understanding the present   59
    Planning ahead   69
Summary – career life planning exercise   76

3   Powerful stress   79
The impact of stress in our lives   78
    Divided loyalties   79

The cost of stress	*81*
How much stress	*81*
Healthy and unhealthy stress	*82*
Practical stress strategies	84
Identifying the sources of stress	*84*
Managing the demands of our time	*86*
Changing the way we see a situation	*103*
Preventing the build-up of pressure	*106*
Changing the response	*108*
Taking care of ourselves so we can cope	*109*
We have only one life – are you in charge?	117
Summary – Practical tips	118

PART II: DEVELOPING PERSONAL POWER — 119

4   Developing inner personal power — 121

What is personal power?	121
Our self-perception	*125*
Our behaviour	*129*
Others' perception	*132*
What can we do to develop personal power?	135
Define and believe in a code of rights and responsibilities	*136*
Stop thinking negatively	*139*
Act with integrity	*151*
Trust our capacity to learn	*152*
Face the spiders in the bath	*153*
Set limits	*155*
Take care of ourselves	*157*
Get the problem out	*159*
Build up a support network	*159*
Minimise contact with negative people	*161*
Think of ourselves as we would of others	*161*
Summary – Practical tips	163

5 Communicating personal power   164

Personal power and behaviour   164
   The importance of respect   164
   Interpersonal power   166
   Our choice in behaviour   167
Different behaviour types   168
   Behaviours and rights   171
   Behaviours and power   172
   Behaving differently   174
Assertion framework   176
   Dealing with a specific problem   176
   Routine use of the framework   193
   Dealing with assertive behaviour   202
Summary – Practical tips   204

PART III: EMPOWERMENT AT WORK   205

6 Maintaining personal power   207

When the going gets tough . . . at work   207
   Being respected is more important
     than being liked   208
Feedback   209
   Giving criticism   211
   Receiving criticism   214
   The benefits of regular feedback   220
Dealing with disciplinary matters   221
   The purpose of disciplinary action   221
Confronting difficult issues   222
   Saying 'no'   223
   Muddle and confusion   227
   Not being heard   228
   Expressing negative feelings   231
   Other people's anger   232
   Bullying   235
   Sexual harrassment   236
When the going gets tough . . . in life   243
   Framework for maintaining personal
     power   246

Summary – Practical tips   247

7 Understanding organisational power 248
Power in organisations   248
What do we mean by power?   249
Why power matters in organisations   251
Organisational politics   252
People and politics   253
What gives us power?   255
Formal power   255
informal power   256
Generating power   258
Who drives the organisation?   259
How do we make progress?   264
Performance   266
Image - does your face fit?   273
Visibility   278
Summary – Practical tips   284

8 Building powerful relationships   285
Why relationships in work matter   285
Networking   286
Barriers to networking   287
The benefits of networking   289
Developing our approach to networking   291
Where to network   293
Doing it . . .   295
Building relationships within the
organisation   299
Managing your manager   300
Working with colleagues   312
Influencing and being influenced   320
Managing a team   322
Other important relationships   325
Summary – Practical tips   332

Bibliography   333

Further Reading   336

When I'm fully in charge of me
I can let you too be free

When I'm using my fullest potential
I can help others do the same

When I'm empowered and strong and sure
I feel neither envious nor threatened

When I can grow at my own rate
I do not fear your taking anything away

I do not fear your overtaking me

(Natasha Josefowitz)

INTRODUCTION

*I myself have never been able to find out
precisely what feminism is: I only know that
people call me a feminist whenever I express
sentiments that differentiate me from a
doormat.*
(Rebecca West)

The Industrial Society has been working in
women's development for more than forty years,
inspired by Elizabeth Pepperell, the namesake
of the Pepperell Management Development
Course for Women. This book is based on the
knowledge, experience and anecdotes of women
who have been involved in the course. We have
both been course participants and have found
its impact on our lives to be significant. We
acknowledge our debt to the women whose con-
tributions have led to the evolution of the course
over the years.

Our focus on women does not imply that
empowerment is an unimportant topic for men,
or that the practical tips might not be relevant
to both sexes. However, we write from a perspective of working with women.

We are aware that we have made generalisa-
tions – about both men and women – that can
be challenged. They are based on observation
and experience and the comments we have
repeatedly heard in our courses; they are not
value judgements and there will always be
exceptions and opposing views.

Neither the course nor this book prescribes how women should behave in the workplace or what they should do with their lives. Instead they aim to help raise awareness of our opportunities and our potential to be fulfilled, and encourage us to take responsibility for our own development.

Sharing experience, learning from others and valuing our own experience are all important themes. The case studies in the book were gathered through a survey of 100 ex-delegates and through interviews with a further 40 (we have changed names and details to protect identities). Their views and experiences are not necessarily ours, but are the real stories of delegates, speakers, tutors and group advisers who have all contributed to the writing of this book. Each one has carried a powerful message of being true and believing in herself. They reveal that the process works if we are prepared to apply our learning.

Both within the course and in the book other women are important – not to be copied or followed, but to inspire and challenge. We are conscious that every woman has her own story to tell, and often we do not know the background or experience that has shaped her decision to take certain actions. Valuing each person's experience helps us to recognise there are no absolute right ways of doing anything and helps us to make choices. With courage, openness and honesty they point us to the answers that are within us.

Caroline

'The key point I have learnt from the Pepperell Development

Course is the adoption of the "forbid if you dare" approach. I have taken on things I did not believe I was really capable of doing, such as applying for a job where it was questionable whether I had the right skills at the time, but trusted in the fact that I could learn as I went along. I have learnt to ask for what I want. The jobs I have really enjoyed have been the ones where I took the risk of approaching the person in charge to see what I could do for them, even though there was no apparent vacancy and getting promoted in the process. The delegates on our courses have taught me over and over again, there is no such thing as "can't do it" but instead we tend to say "won't do it". A direct result from my involvement in the Pepperell Course has been the writing of this book, not because I am a course leader, but because it was too good an opportunity to turn down.

'I have learnt through writing the book that opportunities are incredibly hard work. I have found that I am right to trust my instincts and that I know more than I often give myself credit for. Working in a partnership is all about negotiation, focusing on the achievement of the outcome and working to each person's strengths.'

Eve

'I found my experience of Pepperell very powerful. Much of what was said was common sense – but no one had ever said it before. Listening to others' views and exploring my own opened my eyes, creating an awareness of the steps to take to achieve satisfaction and fulfilment and making sense of what had seemed a muddle, both at work and in my career. As a result I made a career change, started writing books and now run my own business.

'Running the course and working with women has been stimulating, rewarding and empowering. Hearing how they have learnt from and used their experience has kept me going in the long haul to final manuscript, inspiring me to do the same and lifting my energy. Each of the chapters has presented particular

issues to explore from a personal perspective. Working on the book has reminded me that, in common with many women, I can easily underestimate my abilities and knowledge, and talk myself down, and how vitally important it is to work on the things in life that balance and sustain me. It has been good fun, about compromise and sticking with it.'

The book is designed so that each chapter can be read in isolation, as the interest takes you. The short statements in the boxes reflect other women's views and the case studies are their real experiences. The exercises in the tinted boxes can be selected as you chose.

We hope that the Pepperell message – that we have a responsibility to ourselves to fulfil our potential and become all that we are capable of becoming – will support, challenge and encourage you in a personally relevant way.

PART I

EMPOWERMENT – BEGINNING THE PROCESS

1
TAKING RESPONSIBILITY

I believe that we are solely responsible for our choices, and we have to accept the consequences of every deed, word and thought throughout our lifetime
(Elizabeth Kubler-Ross)

WHAT IS THE CHALLENGE?

Empowering ourselves means taking responsibility. This means accepting that we can choose how to respond to everything that happens to us; it means recognising that we can influence the events in our lives. Empowerment means that we generate more of the conditions in our lives that give us satisfaction.

Empowerment is a difficult concept to accept in practice, particularly for women, who are frequently encouraged – and thus learn – not to be ultimately responsible.

> * '*I didn't realise just how much I had let things happen in my life without consciously deciding whether they were what I wanted.*'
> * '*I am always so busy looking after everybody else I don't have time to think about what is important to me.*'
> * '*I felt uncomfortable at the beginning of the course paying all this attention to me. It didn't seem right somehow to*

3

> focus on myself – a bit self-indulgent
> really.'
> * 'I've been brought up to believe that
>   you should respond to what other peo-
>   ple want more than think about what
>   you want.'
> * 'I just did what I was told at work; I didn't
>   think my views would be valuable or
>   valued.'

A lack of personal responsibility will have a significant impact on all aspects of our life.

Marjorie

Marjorie was feeling less than satisfied. 'My job is OK but I have the sense that I could be doing things differently – and gaining more self-fulfilment from my work. I used to be enthusiastic about it, felt creative and determined, but it seems that every suggestion I put forward is met by obstruction. I can't see how to make things happen at work. I'm fighting a losing battle for ideas and resources and it's draining my energy. At the end of a working day I'm going home worn out, with little left to give, which does not do much for my home life either. The family makes demands and the weeks seem to pass frantically by, with no space to think.'

Marjorie found she made no conscious choices about what she wanted to do with her leisure time – indeed made no time for herself. Reflecting on her work and role or looking ahead and making plans were not activities she practised. It seemed that life was scheduled to run like this. She avoided thinking too much about it; 'I'm not unhappy but I've a faint unease that my life is programmed – and not by me.'

Hilary

Reflecting on how she had learnt how to do her new job, Hilary was aware that she had been very influenced by her colleagues' views of how it should be done, based on the previous post holder's style. She had attempted to adapt her own style to that of her predecessor, subverting her preferred approach to that which would please her new team.

Taking their needs and wishes more into account than her own she struggled to be effective. 'I assumed that hers was the best way to go about the task. If I had only trusted my judgement more – and had the confidence to be myself – I would have made my personal mark on the job much more quickly, and achieved the results I wanted with less of a struggle.'

By taking responsibility we can be more fulfilled and more effective in both our life and our career. The women we spoke to frequently cited a greater sense of personal responsibility as an outcome of the Pepperell course. This had a marked and positive effect on their self-confidence.

---

* *'The most important thing I got from the course was an awareness that I was responsible for my own future. I appreciated that it was up to me to create that future by owning the different dimensions of my life.'*
* *'By clarifying what I actually wanted I could then identify a plan to achieve it. By working on it my confidence grew.'*
* *'I realised that it was OK for me to make my own decisions; by allowing other*

> people to make them for me I was in
> fact giving away my power.'
> * 'Saying "no" to the things I really didn't
>   want to do meant that I could focus on
>   the areas that I really enjoy and that will
>   help my career progress.'
> * 'The course changed my life. I came
>   back with confidence and felt prepared
>   to tackle anything. For the first time I
>   believed in myself.'
> * 'It gave me a more secure belief in my
>   abilities; it helped me develop my differ-
>   ences and stop trying to be equal.'

Empowerment underpins the quality of our working life by creating in us greater confidence in our ideas, skills and judgement. It is about knowing ourself and trusting our ability and capacity to do our job positively. Empowered people help to create empowered organisations.

WOMEN'S CAREER EXPERIENCE

Women often underplay their activities and achievements by the ways they describe them. Because in society we have usually defined a career from men's experience, our own careers, by contrast, can seem less important. 'Purposeful', 'directional' and 'driven' are often believed to be prerequisite descriptions of a successful career. Women's career paths, with their variety and sometimes haphazard development, are undervalued in comparison. Because the route

6

is less direct and the experience less sequential, the career itself – and its owner by implication – has a less worthy evaluation.

In this book the word 'career' is used in the broadest sense, encompassing all that we do in our lives – not just paid work but all that occupies us. We view a career as a series of purposeful activities, the unifying feature being the skills, interests and reservoir of different experiences that the owner has acquired. In this definition, diversity adds richness and value.

Lois

'I trained as a nurse as that's what I'd always wanted to be and didn't think beyond marrying a rich man. I went through the usual stages of progression but had to leave because of a back injury. By this time I had had two children and my first marriage had broken up. I couldn't work in nursing but had to earn a living, so I had to transfer my existing skills and learn new ones. Looking back this has been a pattern throughout my career.'

'I only trained in hairdressing as my second husband suggested I buy a hairdressing salon and lent me the money. But I was determined to be financially independent. I didn't make any money beyond a basic living. When the lease ran out I decided to look for something else.

'I was unemployed for three months and desperate for work, when I decided to go temping. I started out as a trainee expediter for an engineering company. They promoted me to supervisor when they realised I had had a substantial amount of experience and was used to a lot of responsibility. Through managing people I learnt about project management and became heavily involved in computing. I worked for a number of years on a contract basis and it was only when my last engineering company relocated that I decided to go temping again.

7

'I realised I loved the environment of the management training consultancy where I was sorting out the database and asked if there were any jobs vacant. The only available position was as an office manager. Although this meant a drop in salary I would be well placed to get promoted. Eventually a position for a consultant with computing skills became vacant for which I successfully applied.

'Since then I have broadened my range of skills to include training. In retrospect I can see how at each stage I brought one set of skills to each career and made a point of acquiring new ones to prepare me for my next move.'

Rebecca

'I was given no guidance at school or at home. I wanted to be an actor and despite being told I could not do it went to drama school, where I met my husband. On leaving college and getting married I started my career as an actor. I worked in rep, toured, had a spell in the West End and was on television. I became pregnant and continued acting even after my child was born.

'Then the guilt became too much and I felt I had to do what was expected of me and became a full-time mother and wife. While I was still at home I started my Open University degree and had my second child. I also worked voluntarily for a charity as a regional organiser setting up retail outlets, where I developed my management skills.

'I started to teach locally on a part-time basis and as the children got older went full time. It wasn't until they were in their teens and my marriage broke up that I decided to start developing my career as a manager at a college of further education. Although I've done a number of different work roles I've always felt my primary responsibility was to be a good mother and wife, even though I had exactly the same training as my husband. I certainly feel that my varied experience has helped me in the job that I do now.'

Career diversity

For women, and now increasingly for men, there is no typical career. Trends indicate that the lives of both men and women will be characterised by a variety of careers. The flexible, 'patchwork' career path that women have typically followed is becoming more familiar and will continue to permeate – for men and women. Professor Charles Handy states in *The Future of Work* that 'it is ironic that just as women have begun to win their fight to lead the kinds of lives that men lead, those lives are beginning to shift towards the pattern from which women are escaping'.

This has been further substantiated be the *Men 2000* (1994) report, which concluded that 'men face an age of uncertainty', because of the need for greater flexibility and less security in patterns of employment to enable organisations to control costs and remain competitive.

Viewing the career as a patchwork offers a positive image, with each square providing different elements contributing to the whole.

The proactive or reactive career?

One differentiating aspect of career experience is the extent to which we drive the career or react to circumstances. Lots of jobs punctuated with periods of other activity (often referred to as career breaks – we prefer the term 'employment break') can reflect a purposefully created career. On the other hand, it could be something that just happens. Similarly a traditional linear career route can seem well organised but

9

can actually be unplanned, encapsulating the 'victim of circumstance' mentality with no sense of personal control.

The key questions are:

- *Do we plan at all?*
- *Do we continue the process of planning?*
- *Do we wait for things to happen?*

WHAT DISEMPOWERS US?

There are many ways in which women are discouraged from empowerment. Although each person's experience is unique, there are some themes that emerge. We might strive to dispel or ignore the differences between men and women, yet characteristic gender roles often influence us in subtle ways. Even if we challenge the existence of stereotypes, our society does encourage sex-specific behaviour. Empowering ourselves demands that we explore and develop our personal understanding of what it means to be a woman in our society today.

THE INFLUENCE OF STEREOTYPES

Stereotypes are communicated through the social images we see all around us: the media, the education process, our families and upbringing and the workplace. Role models – or their lack – in any of these spheres can subtly direct us to think, feel, behave and plan in particular ways – and to reject other options. They set the terms of what is acceptable. The problem with stereotypes is that they can restrict our choices. For example, the idea that men are physically more suited to tasks of strength or that women are more sensitive to emotions can lead us to reject possibilities in our lives and our work.

Social assumptions are rapidly changing. We will still, however, be influenced by those we have absorbed through our lives. Typical myths and fairy tales learnt in childhood encourage us that the female role is to dream, to wait, to search for someone to rescue us or expect someone to care for us. This notion can still exert subtle power, even whilst we actively carve out an independent career. The view that men will be economically active throughout their lives, providing for others and always strong is another example of the types of gender expectations that both sexes can hold. It can be said that, whilst women are disadvantaged in the world of work, men are disadvantaged in the family world.

Women on courses have identified the following examples of expectations that either they hold or others hold for them and that can keep them in a role they do not desire.

Women:
 – are softly spoken
 – care for others
 – always remember and write the birthday cards
 – are available to others
 – organise the family's clothes
 – take responsibility for family festivities

Men:
 – are the constant wage earner

- do not show feelings
- do the car or household maintenance
- are strong in a crisis
- get promoted regularly
- know how to fix technical things

Often these expectations are communicated in subtle ways: the manipulative comment or seemingly innocent question can convey the strength of the belief. Even if we challenge the belief intellectually, those activities we have been trained in can still exert strong power by creating guilt.

Stereotypical gender expectations can often conflict with reality. The financial pressures to work experienced by more women over the last decade (Gallie & White 1993) are at odds with the expectation that women are likely to achieve total satisfaction through devoting their energies to family and childcare. For many, working outside the home is no longer an optional extra. However, the extent to which we change our behaviour to accommodate these contradicted expectations is open to question.

Elaine

Elaine, a middle manager in banking, said: 'I know I don't have to cook every night after a day's work, and my boyfriend often offers, but I feel that I should.'

Carol

Carol, a senior manager in education, described her life as following a very similar pattern to her mother's. 'I run the home, prepare nearly all the meals and take ultimate responsibility for

*the children. The difference is that I have as equally demanding
a job as my husband, whilst her job was the home.'*

GENDER AND CAREER PLANNING

Research in the 1980s amongst secondary
school students identified varying degrees of
emphasis on self-determination in the ways
boys and girls planned their futures. The boys
in this study (Millman 1985) were generally
urged to prepare for the future in an active,
career-focused way, expecting occupational
commitment throughout their lives. On the
other hand, no girl described her future career
without mentioning marriage, motherhood and
childcare arrangements. The future is less pre-
dictable for a young woman, with the possibility
that marriage will determine her place of work
and change her occupation, at least for some
period of her life.

June
*'In my family when we were growing up my brothers's educa-
tion was more important as they were going to be breadwinners
and needed good careers – so they went to boarding school. As
a girl it was assumed that I would be looked after, so I just went
to a day school nearby. I'm single and support myself.'*

Serena
*'We were taught to work hard at school as exam success and a
career were important, but that when we got married – which
we would do – we should give up work to be fulfilled through
raising our families. The real career was the family and this
was the important one. In my experience it hasn't been like
that.'*

13

Gallie and White report that, whilst there is no systematic difference between men and women in their commitment to having a paid job, the focus on employment relative to other life interests is greater for men. An emphasis on different aspects of our lives has often been gender specific; for men the job might well be at the centre whilst women have often been encouraged to put the meeting of others' needs first. Developing our potential – for both sexes – demands that we pay attention to our wishes and plans as individuals, independent of the other roles we might take on, for example of spouse or partner, of mother or daughter, of employee or colleague. Whilst not denying the place of others in our lives or the responsibilities we have accepted, it means keeping a focus on our selves and our life interests.

> ### EXERCISE –
> ### GENDER EXPECTATIONS
>
> * Respond to the following statements. Either discuss them with a partner, or jot down your thoughts alone.
>
>   What is expected of me because I am a woman?
>   How would those expectations be different if I were a man?
> * Consider these expectations in any of the following:
>   - my career
>   - my home life
>   - my personal life

> – my leisure time
> • Consider your own expectations, and
>   those held by significant people in your
>   life, both about you and about them.

COSTS AND BENEFITS

Not taking responsibility means taking a gamble on happiness and satisfaction. If we are not aware of what we want or what is important, we run the risk of not achieving fulfilment. Limited options and lost opportunities are the eventual consequences of not taking responsibility.

There are of course payoffs for not taking responsibility. We can blame others for events – which is easier than making them happen. We do not have to work through the difficulties involved in deciding or doing; we can avoid confronting the big questions about life and meaning. We need not grow up and have the ultimate say in our own lives.

Giving up personal power can mean wasting your life. Imagine a deathbed scene, looking back on your life and regretting how it has been spent. Life is not a dress rehearsal. The challenge is to maintain or take back some control of our lives to maximise our satisfaction. The benefits are in achieving the things that fulfill us and that square with our values.

Sally

Approaching 40, Sally wondered if there wasn't more to life than daily commuting to her responsible, demanding and fulfilling middle-management public service job. 'Driving around the M25 every day I began to wonder if there weren't more

15

important things for me to be doing. In the past I had tended to play safe but I don't want to regret that I've missed out on what I really want.'

Her decision to leave, move abroad, explore a change of career direction and risk financial insecurity was based on her desire to spend a lot of time with her partner – someone she cared a lot about. 'I realised that the big decisions are OK to make. Facing uncertainty is OK. I'm more self assured that I will cope, I don't want to waste any more time – it's precious. Go for the best– and enjoy it!'

WHAT STOPS US TAKING RESPONSIBILITY?

Obstacles to even beginning to take responsibility for our lives can be externally or internally created and reflect our experience of femininity. The ways we have learnt how to lead our lives could well have incorporated some of the following.

DO I HAVE A CHOICE?

The more we feel the possibilities in our lives will be influenced by others, the less inclined we will be to plan our careers. At its simplest this is about keeping options open; at its most significant it is giving away our power.

- Do we avoid taking action because it might prevent other possibilities?
- Do we refuse to choose because we are more concerned about other people, subverting our choices to their choices?
- Do we believe that someone else will take the lead and make decisions, taking ultimate responsibility?

This is the 'pinball machine' perspective: the movement created might lead to success or it might not – but the movement is random, has its own momentum and is out of control. It is accompanied by the sense that we do not have the right or the power to control our own lives.

THINKING NEGATIVELY ABOUT THE FUTURE

Often we find all kinds of reasons for not changing a situation that does not fulfil us. To take a hard look at what we want in the future can be frightening and demanding – and clearly we will be disappointed if we do not get it. The perceived outcome – often in the negative – stops us taking action. 'I'm bound to fail' is a potent line.

There are other ways of focusing on the future that limit us. The thought: 'It will be different when' can keep us inactive. For example:

'It will be different when
 – we move house
 – the kids are older
 – I lose weight
 – my boss leaves
 – the company is doing better'

These expressions, often not explicitly stated, allow us to focus on a distant time before which we can take no action. Because the future is out of our control this keeps us static.

The belief that time in the future is too limited to merit any effort acts as a block to action for many women. The following views can be held at varying ages – from 25 to 75!

* *I'm too old for this.*

17

*   *No one will appoint me at my age.*
*   *It's not worth my changing now.*

Contrast Marie's view: 'At 55 I feel that my career is really taking off now', while Alice entered teaching at 45 and attained a headship by the age of 55.

Facing the future with no sense of direction can be scary and keep us inactive. Innumerable possibilities can make the choice difficult; having no idea of where we are going makes moving in a purposeful way impossible. Choices reflect who we are, and often we will have lost sight of that. Planning for the future needs to be based on a clear sense of values and priorities which fuel the vision. This is covered in detail in Chapter 2.

FOCUSING ON THE PAST

By considering all the 'if onlys' we can similarly keep ourselves safe through inactivity. The following examples might be familiar.

'If only I :

- – hadn't failed my last exam
- – hadn't stayed in this job too long
- – hadn't wasted career time in that last move
- – had had my children earlier/later
- – had not got married when I did
- – had worked harder at my career before now'

By looking back we absolve ourselves from any responsibility for our present situation and justify our inactivity with compelling arguments.

18

The messages we received in the past about our capabilities can limit our choices, and the ways we speak of ourselves can maintain this negative perspective. This stops us moving forward.

Grace

'I did not have a natural aptitude for maths at school. This was reinforced by my parents sympathetically telling me I was no good at it. It became natural for me to say I was hopeless at figures because I genuinely believed it . . . to the extent I would rather someone else take responsibilty than even have a go. Obviously for me to progress as a manager this attitude had to be challenged. One boss who saw budgeting as my responsiblity carefully built my confidence and allowed me to discover I could handle figures. To stop believing the negative message I had to stop saying "I'm no good."'

19

Feeling positive about the fact that things have always turned up in the past can be another reason we wait for things to happen. Sometimes they do and sometimes they do not; we can still take advantage of them even if we are on the move. We disempower ourselves if chance is the only option.

BEING TOO BUSY IN THE PRESENT

Women often learn to take care of everyone else and do not devote energy to looking after for themselves. Clearly the role of wife and mother can be immensely satisfying but it does not necessarily suit everyone, nor will it last a life-time. Keeping the focus on the home and being the support system for others means we have little time to participate in the world outside.

Without undermining the value of what we do to occupy us, busy-ness and activity can distract us from taking time for recharging activities and we run the risk of losing sight of who we are. Some women report that they no longer know what is important to them or what they want out of life. Before we can take a decision to make things happen we need space to think.

Patricia

'It was easy to fall into the single career woman trap: working long hours in a demanding high-pressure job, cramming in social engagements to ensure I kept up with my friends, fitting in domestic essentials to keep me going, booking holidays away to take advantage of my leave. It was on an unexpectedly free day during a business trip that I realised that every minute of my life was scheduled and filled. There was no time to stop and think – did I want all this?'

By consistently not listening to what we want or think, we diminish our capacity to keep in touch with it. Not being clear about what drives us obstructs our progress. A deep sense of personal values goes hand in hand with empowerment. Each of us places a different emphasis on the things that are important in our life and work. Finding work that fuels our sense of values and allows their expression is an important step in the empowering process.

Debbie

'As a teenager I was very gifted at drama and art and had a mentor who urged me to pursue my talent. However, because I could speak five languages, my grandparents, who were responsible for me, insisted I go to finishing school and learn to type. All my creative instinct was stifled. I sailed through the course, achieved excellent qualifications and for a number of years had extremely well-paid jobs as an international interpreter and personal assistant to some very high-powered people. In a sense that became the trap.

'I met my husband and worked with him, again earning a lot of money in the field of sales and marketing. At the time I was desperately unhappy so I tried even harder to do well and became a trophy wife and supermum in the process. I worked hard at entertaining clients. Over a period of time I began to burn out completely and ended up in a treatment centre. I had to take stock of where I was in my life and realised for a very long time I had been in chronic conflict with my values. I am now using all of my creative talent working as a therapist. It has been a painful journey but one worth travelling.'

THE EFFECT IT WOULD HAVE ON OTHERS

Taking responsibility requires courage and great
thought. We need to recognise that changing one

21

EXERCISE – PERSONAL VALUES

- The following are some of the things that you may value. Think about each one in turn and rate it on the scale 1 (low) to 10 (high), putting a tick in the appropriate column

VALUE	Low 1	2	3	4	5	6	7	8	9	High 10
Achieving your goals										
Adventure										
Affection										
Being creative										
Competing with others										
Co-operating with others										
Financial security										
Family happiness										
Freedom										
Friendship										
Getting on										
Having inner harmony										
Health										
Improving society										
Integrity										
Involvement										
Loyalty										
Order										
Personal development										
Recognition										
Religion										
Responsibility										
Self-respect										
Wealth										
Wisdom										

Source: Ryan (1986).

- When you have worked through this list, add any other values that are important to you and rate them too.

thing can have a fundamental impact on other aspects of our life.

For example the people in our lives may be used to us always thinking of them first, or have an expectation that our life will follow the path they have prescribed for us. If we choose to go against their perception they can feel hurt, disillusioned or even disappointed. We have to question whether what other people want for us is appropriate.

If the answer is 'no', are we prepared to take the risk of fulfilling our potential in a way that suits us as individuals and let go of the expectations of other people in our lives? For some of us the price might seem too high to pay and yet by being true to what we really consider of value we are more likely to have the life we've always wanted.

Frances

Frances had been a housewife for ten years looking after her children. When they left primary school she decided the time had come for her to fulfil her dream of studying for a degree. 'At first my husband was really supportive. When I realised for the first time I was intelligent, that I had skills that could be developed and opinions of my own, we started to fall out. The arguments really intensified when I decided I wanted a career of my own, financial independence and a say on how the finances were managed in the home. It dawned on me that he did not want me to be my own person, independent of my role as a mother and wife. It is really sad but we had to split up. I felt I could no longer be the person I was. I would not have been true to myself.'

Lydia

Lydia's sister was always late when they met. Eventually Lydia decided she would tell her sister how annoying she

23

found it and that she was not prepared to wait longer than fifteen minutes. The next time she waited for fifteen minutes, and then left. Her sister was really angry at first and it created a temporary atmosphere between them, but she was never late again.

LINKS WITH SELF-ESTEEM

Looking on ourselves positively is an integral part of the development process. Unfortunately it is so much easier to focus on the things we do less well or that we do not feel good about. Regularly talking ourselves down has the effect of keeping us looking at the negative and feeling negative. It can seem unacceptable to reverse the trend and acknowledge and applaud the positive. All sorts of reasons why we should not do this will come to mind.

* *I'd be bragging.*
* *Nice girls don't sell themselves.*
* *Doesn't everyone do it like this?*
* *Well I should do it well, it's what I'm paid for.*

The ways in which we view ourselves and what happens in our lives are intricately connected (and explored more fully in Chapter 4).

We might consistently evaluate ourselves negatively in relation to others, attributing to them the skill or composure that we feel we lack. We assume that they are more confident, skilled or knowledgeable than us. The process of negative comparison reinforces a sense of inadequacy which helps keep us disempowered and hinders the task of making choices.

Taking responsibility for ourselves and the consequences of our actions inevitably involves changes to self-perception and thus self-esteem. To take control of our self-esteem is a significant choice in itself, for it moves us away from the 'victim' mentality that gives our power to others.

To a far greater extent than men, women are commonly taught to link their self-esteem with what other people think of them, whereas men will more commonly either equate self-esteem with achievement or be fuelled by a greater sense of self-worth. Whereas men are encouraged to see freedom and self-reliance as valuable characteristics, women learn to value an ability to give love and be loved and to respond to the needs of others. At the centre of empowering ourselves is learning to be the judge of our own worth.

Fear can be a significant obstacle. It can arise from lack of knowledge or unfamiliarity and often it will be accompanied by a focus on the reasons why we cannot do something, rather than on the steps to do it. The extent to which we allow the fear to paralyse us will be related to our self-esteem – the two are interdependent. This book will give practical suggestions and tips that other women have found helpful in taking control.

Elizabeth

Elizabeth believes there are distinct advantages to being a woman. 'If we constantly look at the disadvantages we will only see the negative and feel like a victim. Women have many advantages that need to be valued, for example it is acceptable to be a homemaker and spend time with the children. We are

25

really fortunate because we can express and release our emotions and generally have a more powerful network of support through having closer intimate friendships than our male counterparts. A final advantage for some of us could be that if we work in a place where they have low expectations it means we have plenty of opportunity to prove ourselves!'

DECIDING TO CHANGE

THE PEPPERELL BOX

Elizabeth Pepperell described the ways we keep ourselves safe and not challenged by determining in our own minds the extent of our capabilities. These limits are represented by the walls of the Pepperell Box. Each person will have different limits.

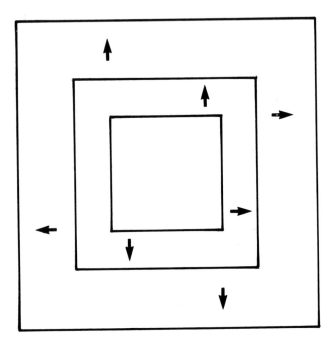

Elizabeth Pepperell believed that once we start to push back the boundaries it is possible to keep going – the only limits being:

- our perception of ourself and our capabilities

- our aspirations.

Before we can do this, we need to recognise the boundaries – the boxes we are in. It can be useful to appreciate where the messages that keep us in the safe zone come from. They usually reflect our sense of entitlement and can thus be self-limiting.

---

*   *'No one has ever job shared before so why should they allow me?'*

*   *'I thought that I must regularly get promotion to indicate progress in my career.'*

*   *'It is a problem to change my job because it is so secure.'*

*   *'I thought that confidence was something you either had or did not have, rather than it coming from facing the things you're scared of.'*

*   *'I thought that someone else could tell me what to do with my career.'*

*   *'Because I was well paid it was difficult to step into something that wasn't but which would ultimately fulfil me.'*

*   *'I thought that I should give up my job to manage the family.'*

> *   *'I thought I should carry on working after my children were born because that's what women of the nineties do, isn't it?'*
> *   *'I thought his career was more important than mine.'*
> *   *'I didn't realise I could ask for training; I thought they should know what I needed.'*

One way to keep ourselves in the boxes is by avoiding risk. Empowerment, because it involves exercising choice and improving the quality of our lives, can involve taking risks. The challenge is not only to push back the boundaries, but to determine for ourselves which boundaries to extend. Getting back in touch with what motivates and is important to us will help in deciding what areas of our lives are to be tackled. Once we have made the choices about what to challenge, the rest is relatively easy.

WHAT DOES SUCCESS MEAN TO ME?

It is common for women to see high-quality interpersonal relationships and close affiliation with others as more important than their individual accomplishments. However, a desire to be liked by everyone will always be disappointed; just as we do not like all people equally, so not everyone will like us. Whilst good relationships are important, it is more important that we like our selves rather than behave in ways that compromise ourselves or our values and our self-esteem.

Success needs to be defined in our own terms. Other peoples' expectations of what it should mean to us can affect our own view, until over time we do not know what we do want out of life. Parental, social, educational, male and female perceptions will to a greater or lesser extent colour our own sense of self and this in turn affects our belief in our capabilities.

Julie

'I had been separated for three years and wasn't too sure where my life was going. I had had to move out of my house and learn to live by myself. I was looking to work to provide me with the focus of my life. I didn't know what the choices were for me at this late stage of a working life. I didn't realise that it was up to me to create my own definition of success and yet when I started to sort out the priorities I found it great fun and worked on developing my personal life.'

It is important to recognise our uniqueness. Everyone has a different definition of success. We can look at others and take what suits us but not use their experience as a blueprint. Taking the aspects of others' experience we like and rejecting the bits we do not like is empowering.

> ### *Success to me is:*
>
> * *'Being comfortable with what I am doing and sticking by my values and principles.'*
> * *'Enjoying my work and learning new things within it.'*
> * *'Taking two holidays a year.'*
> * *'Having time to see my friends.'*
> * *'Earning enough not to worry.'*
> * *'Passing my examinations.'*
> * *'Reaching a senior position in my organisation.'*
> * *'Being respected as an expert in my field.'*
> * *'Having children and raising them as well as I can.'*
> * *'Launching a new product.'*
>   *'Being in charge of my organisation and making an impact on it.'*
> * *'Leaving an unsatisfactory relationship.'*
> * *'Good health.'*
> * *'Buying the clothes that make me feel good.'*
> * *'Negotiating the salary increase I feel I deserve.'*

EXERCISE– SUCCESS

* Ask yourself:

What does success mean to me?

One way we can learn and progress is by talking to people who inspire and challenge us. We can grow in self-knowledge if we recognise what stimulates us or what it is we admire and per-haps aspire to. Role models can broaden our horizons by telling us what is possible and per-haps challenging what we feel to be the impossible.

We can disempower ourselves by:

- *shutting our minds to others' experience*
- *habitually comparing ourselves unfavourably to others*
- *assuming that it was easy for them*
- *trying to become someone we are not*
- *accepting that what others say or do is what we should say or do*
- *restricting our notion of what is acceptable for someone like us*

For positive benefit we should:

- *seek exposure to a broad range of role models*
- *be selective about what we take from their experience*
- *actively seek contact with those that inspire us*
- *limit our contact with those who negatively affect our sense of potential*
- *allow ourselves to learn from others, their experience and views*
- *become a role model for others and give some-thing back*

SUMMARY –
PRACTICAL TIPS

* Recognise that you can influence events in your life
* Identify your own wishes and plans, independent of the other roles you have in relation to others
* Challenge limiting expectations
* Value your unique career path and think of it in a purposeful way
* Consider what you want to have achieved before you die
* Stop dwelling on the obstacles to progress and focus on the opportunities
* Clarify your values and priorities
* Identify the boundaries that prevent you from moving forward
* Consider what success means to you
* Talk to people who inspire you
* Trust your judgement

2
EYES ON THE HILLS, FEET ON THE GROUND

*A liberated woman is one who feels confident
in herself, and is happy in what she is doing.
She is a person who has a sense of self . . . It
all comes down to freedom of choice.*
(Betty Ford)

CAREER AND LIFE PLANNING

'What will you do when you grow up?' is a question that often provokes a blank reaction. Unsure of what we really do want, we grasp at the more obvious occupations or copy the routes our parents have taken. What we fail to see is that a career or a job of paid work is really an extension of ourselves and should fit into our lives, changing as we change.

The beliefs and assumptions that we hold about life and the course it will take, possibly more unconscious than conscious, will determine how we approach our lives.

> * '*I do not think of my life following a straightforward route, rather it being a hotch potch of experiences which I need to be open to respond to.*'

* *'My life is really mapped out and its structure determines the decisions I make. There are certain things we all do and I will be no exception.'*
* *'I can really choose exactly what it is I do with my life – I will make the decisions and not leave them to chance.'*
* *'I will plan but I know that I'll change my plans if the right man comes along or something happens at work.'*
* *'I let life take its course until events force a reaction.'*
* *'I like to have plans for what I will do in the next year, next five and next ten years.'*
* *'When I was a teenager and during my twenties it was important to think ahead. I feel that the decisions I made then stopped me making any more major ones.'*
* *'I used to plan, but so many difficult things have happened that I've had to deal with that now I don't.'*

To begin the process of taking responsibility for our own career we need to be able to pull these beliefs from the unconscious into the conscious, question them and test out their validity in our own reality. Do we really believe this, or is it an inherited belief or value adapted from our parents or peers?

When asked, most people will deny that much in their lives has been planned. Even women who have been moving purposely along a clear path will attribute their achievements to luck, or report that they were in the right place at the right time. This at worst denies or at best undermines the part we play in our lives. Whilst accepting there may be elements of chance in our experience, a more accurate view is that luck occurs when preparation meets opportunity. Being clear that we are searching or focused on what we want can have a remarkable impact on events and our reaction to them.

Career life planning is based on self-knowledge and an ability to be flexible in our response to chance and unexpected opportunity. With personal preference we can vary the degree to which we set goals and work towards them, equipped to respond more powerfully to change and ultimately to direct it. It is not a rigid and inflexible process.

LIFE AS A PROCESS OF CHANGE

However powerful we feel in determining the course of our lives, planning to achieve what we want is a life-long process, not something that we will do just once. In today's climate, flexibility and the ability to respond to change, coupled with the commitment to drive one's one path, are the currency of success. These qualities also maximise personal satisfaction and future opportunity.

Certain life stages demand more planning – either formally or informally. For example:

- making a career choice or change
- entering or leaving a relationship
- getting qualifications

- having a family
- moving house or area
- facing redundancy
- facing retirement

After such periods of change there is a need for consolidation.

There will be times in our lives when events themselves can lead us, or when we are contented as we are. At other times unforeseen circumstances can demolish carefully made plans. We need to be able to respond in the most positive ways possible for us. This is helped if we know what is important to us.

---

* *Corinne decided to go to college – to study for a degree. She arranged part-time work to help finance it.*
* *Angie decided to leave an unsatisfactory relationship.*
* *Gemma bought a piano as she had always loved playing as a child.*
* *Megan went for a major promotion and became the most senior woman in her organisation.*
* *Tess got involved in local politics.*
* *Carmen set up her own business.*
* *Ewa wanted international experience and went to work abroad.*
* *Siobhan left the city she worked in to live in the country.*

> * *Suzanne made a decision to resign from two working parties that would develop her career, in order to have more time at home.*
> * *Fleur rejoined the badminton club to have more fun and help manage her stress.*
> * *Annabel employed a cleaner and stopped cooking for friends.*

TAKING TIME

Career life planning is energy intensive and slow. Because there are no simple answers it is often avoided.

Career life planning involves time:

- to review our experience
- to reflect on what is important in our lives
- to determine our values
- to clarify our aspirations
- to decide on short-term action
- to set long-term goals
- to review our progress

Focusing attention on what is important is helped if we value ourself highly enough to give ourself time, balancing it with other people's demands on our time. This in turn helps us feel good about ourself. As we recognise and accept our strengths, clarify our skills and interests and confront our weaknesses we gain greater self-acceptance, clarity and confidence. We are also able to recognise those opportunities where we can apply and maximise our skills and strengths and minimise our weaknesses.

37

Tara

Tara went to career counselling because she was unhappy in her job in the civil service. Ater just two sessions she realised that it wasn't the job that was the problem, it was her life. 'I had spent years on the treadmill – progressing my career, buying a house, getting the mortgage – because that's what everyone does. Carrying on because of the "oughts", because of how I was brought up I suppose. I decided to give myself time out to think about what I want, to give myself a break and some space. I'm selling my house and then I'm using the money to finance going away, probably for a year, to stand back from it all. I think I would have gone mad if I didn't do this. I'm going against everything but I need to be true to myself.'

Jasmin

Jasmin changed her career. 'I was really unhappy as an accountant and found the work totally draining. The only thing that helped me forget it and recover my energy were my window boxes and tiny patio garden. I enjoyed them so much I wondered if I could make a career change. First I did an evening class in gardening where I learnt about plants; the next year another on garden design. I read up on starting a small business, did some work for friends and contacts at weekends and eventually took the plunge to go it alone. I love my work as a garden designer now.'

Whilst the exercises in this chapter are themselves very simple, the work we need to do to complete them is not, exposing as it does our dreams and desires and the extent to which we achieve them. It can be extremely hard to exercise the choices we have and harder still to make them. Whatever the degree of difficulty it is useful to understand that the exercises provide a framework for information-gathering and action that can help us in a number of ways:

- building self-esteem and confidence
- clarifying life priorities
- changing self perception and influencing others' perceptions
- making major life changes
- identifying the next career move
- preparing a CV or job application
- preparing for interview

CAREER DEVELOPMENT FRAMEWORK

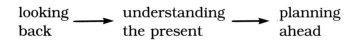

looking back → understanding the present → planning ahead

The framework for career develoment identifies the three main stages of activity and focus. We cannot move forwards without information, acquired from understanding of the past and awareness of the present. We need answers to the following questions:

- **Looking back**
  What *skills* and *strengths* have you acquired or developed?
  What have been the high spots, and the low spots?
  What experience and knowledge could you transfer?
- **Understanding the present**
  How is your job/work role at present?
  What are you enjoying, and not enjoying?
  Is there appropriate challenge and opportunity for you?
- **Planning ahead**
  In what directions might you go?

What are your long- and short-term goals?
How will you achieve them?

LOOKING BACK

Looking back involves reviewing our career to date as a basis for identifying our skills and appreciating our strengths. We can clarify our interests and gain insight into what motivates and demotivates us by remembering when we felt positive, inspired and enthusiastic. By diagnosing the cultures we have flourished and floundered in, we can begin to appreciate the working conditions which most suit us and come to understand our personal value system.

Career review

The career review is a good way to get the whole picture. It can help highlight what we have achieved and can build confidence by helping us value ourselves. It might also create feelings of discomfort or sadness that relate to previous experience.

EXERCISE – CAREER REVIEW

- On a large sheet of paper plot out your career to date. Use colours, shapes and words to represent it visually.
  Include:
  – the main activities that you have been involved in (paid and unpaid)

– major decision times and the path chosen
– the high spots and the low points for you
Start at an appropriate time for you (this is often when leaving school or full-time education) and go up to the present. Please note that there is no right or wrong way to do this and it is not an exercise in art or design!

Do not spend too long on this – about half an hour is normally the maximum. The next stage is more lengthy.

• Review your career using the following triggers (it is important to have a supportive listening friend or colleague with whom to talk through this vital stage of the exercise):
– What are you proud of?
– What have you overcome?
– What made the high spots and the low spots?
– Do any patterns emerge?
– What do you see as your personal strengths illustrated through your experience?
– What working environments have you flourished or floundered in?

We may see a variety of moves – both in and out of the workplace, and in a range of roles and activities within it. The resulting jumble can

41

seem less valuable because it does not seem to have any unifying theme or represent tangible growth of achievement, skill or responsibility. Yet the experience, interests and transferable skills are the threads that make the whole a positive asset.

Identifying transferable skills

Often women will think that they cannot do a particular job because they do not have the relevant experience. Although knowledge and experience are useful, it is the skills we have developed in the past that are at the centre of any work.

A skill is an ability that can be acquired or learnt (e.g. balancing books or using a computer), or is an expression of our innate abilities that improves with experience (e.g. managing a team, solving problems or thinking strategically). Skills – or the results of skills – are generally revealed in our actions and so can be observed to a certain extent. For example, a finished report displays written communication, organising of material and probably research skills. Skills can be developed to varying degrees, usually improve with practice and can be transferred into new contexts. A belief in our skill base equips us to choose and implement new routes.

Lucy
Lucy felt that as a teacher she was not really equipped to tackle any other work and confused the difficulties inherent in a career change with her own lack of potential. 'It was only when I analysed my skills and saw how I had used them in a variety

of contexts – managing a team project, organising a depart-
ment, presenting information to groups of pupils and parents,
editing a magazine and publicity sheet and implementing new
initiatives, that I had more confidence in my ability to make the
change to campaigning within a management consultancy.
Appreciating the skills required in the new role and checking
them against mine was what made the difference. It's easy to
feel overwhelmed with your lack of directly relevant experience
and knowledge, but that can always be learnt. It's the skills
that mean you can do the job or not.'

EXERCISE – SKILLS REVIEW

- Using your career review, identify and list the skills you
  have developed throughout your career. This can be difficult; if you are not sure of your skills use the following
  checklist to help.

TYPES OF SKILL	SKILLS I HAVE WITH EXAMPLES OF WHERE DEMONSTRATED IN MY CAREER
NUMERICAL Examples: keeping accounts, managing money, working out measurements, estimating, using maths to solve problems, monitor performance or make predictions	

VERBAL COMMUNICATION
Examples: teaching, selling,
using the telephone,
answering queries, public
speaking, advising

**WRITTEN
COMMUNICATION**
Examples: writing letters,
reports, or minutes,
understanding and
interpreting reports,
checking or revising written
material

MENTAL SKILLS
Examples: solving problems
logically or creatively, taking
in facts and figures for later
use, analysing data,
developing good ideas,
seeing solutions

COMPUTER SKILLS
Examples: using software,
keyboard skills, creating
software

**ORGANISATIONAL/
ADMINISTRATIVE**
Examples: keeping files and
records, organising people,
setting up systems, dealing

with paperwork and correspondence, gathering information

MANAGEMENT SKILLS
Examples: motivating people, planning, co-ordinating, monitoring performance, delegating, allocating resources, achieving results with others, anticipating problems, translating ideas into reality

---

LEADERSHIP SKILLS
Examples: directing people, strategic planning, setting goals and moving people towards them, making decisions, practical understanding of the impact of trends

---

INTERPERSONAL SKILLS
Examples: team working, influencing people, communicating with a range of people, coaching, facilitating, listening, counselling, resolving conflict, running meetings, advising people

SELF-MANAGEMENT
SKILLS
Examples: prioritising,
using time appropriately,
stress management,
personal and work
organisation, career
planning

MECHANICAL
Examples: operating
machines, repairing and
identifying faults to
electrical, technological and
mechanical equipment

PRACTICAL
Examples: building,
decorating, sewing,
gardening, constructing,
physical activity, practical
problem-solving

ARTISTIC/CREATIVE
SKILLS
Examples: creating,
analysing, applying or
appreciating music, drama,
the visual arts, literature

SCIENTIFIC SKILLS
Examples: applying
scientific principles to

problems, generating new
approaches

TECHNICAL SKILLS
Write in here any other
specific technical skills you
have that are not included
above

OTHERS
Write in here any other
skills you have that are not
under the above headings

• Circle the skills you
  think are your best ones.
  Underline the ones you
  most enjoy using.

The importance of interesting work

In addition to appreciating the skills that are our
base for work, we need an understanding of the
type and nature of work that interests us. Usually
we will have a number of interest areas with one
or two stronger preferences. However, some of us
may have lost touch with our likes and dislikes
as a result of either very broad or rather limited
experience of working. It can often help to elim-
inate the things that definitely do not interest us.
Clarity of what interests us can fire action.

Asking ourselves what we really enjoyed and
what gave us the most satisfaction is one way to
unravel the jumble of a varied career. However

small the example, particularly of what we really disliked, we should note it down. A pattern will emerge that will help in reinforcing and adding to our skills.

<u>EXERCISE –</u>
<u>WHAT INTERESTS ME?</u>

- Review and clarify your interests by looking back at those aspects of your career or working life that you have enjoyed and those that you have not enjoyed. Extend your thinking outside your career, looking at personal interests and hobbies. (Remember Jasmin who made her hobby into her career with the help of formal training.)
- Rate the interest on a scale of 1–5 with 5 as high-level interest. To help, you could illustrate the ways you have exercised the interest with activities on the following checklist.

INTEREST GROUPS	MY INTEREST 1 ---------- 5	THINGS I'VE DONE
NATURAL (caring for animals, plants, resources)		
MECHANICAL (using machinery, understanding mechanics)		
PRACTICAL (using strength and skill to build and repair)		

OUTDOOR
(being out and about,
physically active)

_____

ARTISTIC
(music, art, design, beauty,
theatre)

_____

VERBAL
(languages, written or
spoken words)

_____

NUMERICAL
(working with figures)

_____

CLERICAL
(organising paperwork)

_____

ENTERPRISING
(leading or convincing
others, meeting
people, generating new
initiatives)

_____

GENERAL SERVICE
(providing a service)

_____

PEOPLE
(advising, understanding,
managing and helping
people)

SCIENTIFIC/
INVESTIGATIVE
(solving problems,
discovering facts)

- Write down on a separate sheet any other interests that have not been covered.
- Go through the lists and circle the most important ones for you.

Learning from experience

Patterns may well emerge from the career review. How we interpret them and use the information is significant. David Kolb believed that learning from experience follows a four-stage cycle: experience, on reflection, is translated into concepts or theories that, when applied, form the basis for future activity. In order for learning to be fully integrated we need to move round the cycle; sometimes we get stuck and do not complete the process. Faulty learning also occurs when we draw false conclusions, fail to understand, or do not act on the application.

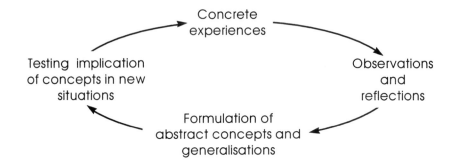

Most of the time we do not need to think about how we learn. However, we will usually have developed beliefs about our capabilities, for example our ability to succeed in certain tasks, work at a particular level or learn specific subject areas. As a result of this we may well have a low self-perception of our potential that influences our thinking about the future. Assuming, for example, that 'I'm not intelligent', 'I'm no good at learning new things', 'My career has been useless' or 'I have no valuable skills', can limit our ability to attempt new things. To generate new ways of achieving objectives we have to let go of such beliefs.

Penny
Because she had had a variety of different jobs Penny believed that no employer would take her application seriously as she lacked long experience in one field. She learnt to recognise that her skills and breadth of experience could be viewed positively – but she had to do so herself before anyone else would.

Sheila
Sheila thought that it was useless applying for promotion because she had not been shortlisted in her previous five applications. She believed her career had ended. When she sought advice from a senior colleague she recognised that she could improve her written applications, gain feedback from the recruitment manager and match herself more closely to the person specification. She arranged a practice interview when she got shortlisted and got a post she wanted.

Learning from the lows

Finding positive learning points in all experience, however negative, is a natural strength which can be lost or clouded by the strong emotion. Our previous experience – and our reactions to it – can lead us to believe that we are not empowered. We might well have absorbed family myths about what is not possible as well as being subject to real organisational, sexist, racist or ageist barriers. However, we have to appreciate that we can make a difference – not necessarily to circumstances but to the way we handle them.

The most difficult times in our lives often contain the key to increased self-awareness and empowerment. Understanding how we coped, what we did well and where we failed can help to identify both positive and negative reactions that have influenced our self-image and aided or blocked our decision. Recognising the need for change can be a powerful and valuable spur to development and action.

Sometimes the lows are imposed on us by others or occur by disaster or outside influence.

---

* *Redundancy*
* *Reorganisation at work, ongoing threat of redundancy*
* *Serious illness*
* *Family problems such as dealing with a difficult adolescent, long-term care of elderly relatives, unresolved childcare demands*
* *Bereavement*
* *Divorce or relationship breakdown*
* *Failed exams*

---

* *Major error at work*
* *Repeated rejection in applications*
* *Home destroyed by fire*
* *Serious car accident*
* *Persistent bullying and harassment*
* *Long-term unemployment*
* *Extreme unhappiness in role or organisation*

In some circumstances it may be our own behaviour or actions that keep us in the lows; in this case, identifying what stops us from changing is an important step.

Zoe

Zoe was made redundant. 'I felt frightened, angry and insecure. I got involved in a group of people in the same position and we did a lot of moaning about the company and commiserating with each other. This was important for me but I realised that I had to take steps to help myself. Eventually I got a grip of myself and enquired if there were other positions coming up in the company. On this information I targeted specific departments, used all my contacts and finally was interviewed for a trainee post in marketing, albeit at a lower status – which I obtained. What I learned was that I have transferable skills, I can speak up for myself when necessary and that I am valued by the company. I also appreciate the importance of asking for help and accepting support from my colleagues and friends.'

Managing personal change is always difficult and can be painful; even welcome change involves adjustment and pressure. However, by finding the strengths and learning points in our past experience we can prepare more effectively for change.

53

EXERCISE –
LEARNING FROM PERSONAL CHANGE

- Identify a situation in which you experienced major change, in either your personal or your professional life. This can be change initiated by you or that you had to respond to.

- Ask yourself:

  What happened?
  How did I feel?
  What actions did I take?
  What was the outcome?
  What alternative action could I have taken?

- What positive learning conclusions can I draw from this?
  What personal qualities and characteristics did I display?

Helps and hindrances

Externally imposed personal change can either help or hinder career development. Similarly, in any change process we may well encounter obstacles that impede our progress. There will also be things that help us, but these are often more obscure. It is vital to look with fresh eyes at what we can and cannot change.

The more self-aware we are, the more readily we can turn a negative situation into a positive opportunity. We may not be able to change the external situation but we can change our inner reaction and way of dealing with it, which is how

we grow and move forwards. In this way perceived obstacles actually help us.

---

*   'I worked in three colleges that either closed down or amalgamated, so I was forced to move. Each time I got a pro-moted post.'
*   'My partner was relocated. After strug-gling to see each other at weekends I decided to give up my job and move to be with him. I realised this was an opportunity for me to retrain as an illus-trator which is something I've always wanted to do.'
*   'I was threatened with redundancy. I made a point of telling all my business contacts and one of them offered me the job I now enjoy.'

It is easy to dwell on what we cannot do rather
than focusing on what we can do. Being clear
about our major personal achievements in the
past helps us to appreciate what we are capable
of achieving in the future. From them we can
learn more about what drives us and identify
our personal strengths (our internal helps).
Connecting with the energy that accompanies
achievements and letting it fuel the future is
an empowering tool. It also shifts the focus from
the negatives to the positives. Positive self-
knowledge also helps us recognise and tackle
our weaknesses (our internal hindrances)
without letting them destabilise or paralyse
us.

Val

Val asked two people that she trusted to list her strengths and weaknesses. One was a senior male colleague, the other a female friend and ex-flatmate. 'The lists were remarkably similar,' she said. 'I started work to address my weaknesses, steadily reducing their impact with the aim of eliminating them. When the time was right to discuss promotion again with my boss I showed him the lists and explained what I had been doing. He was really surprised and impressed that I had been so proactive and determined.'

Although each person's list will be different, the helps and hindrances in our career development will be either internal or external to us, and thus subject to varying degrees of control.

Internal hindrances

- a skills deficiency
- a lack of relevant knowledge or experience
- personal characteristics or tendencies such as procrastination, indecision, focusing on the negative
- not knowing what we want
- low self-image or low confidence

Internal helps

- skills
- personal strengths
- qualifications
- subject-specific knowledge
- positive self-image and confidence
- life experiences

Rachel

Rachel, a staff nurse, was disciplined at work because of a serious mistake. 'At the disciplinary hearing it emerged very clearly that there had been a significant lack of training and support. The whole ward was stressed out. I was asked to go back to the same hospital but a different department. The attitude of my new colleagues was extremely hostile and I was treated as someone who could not be trusted. The experience made me review my whole career. I realised I loved nursing and wanted to continue.

'I could manage my way out of the situation or run away from the problem. I chose to face the problem head on and started really focusing on working as a team player, not reacting to the hostility. In time the key problem people left and I established good working relations with all of the staff. It's taken me five years but I am now the manager of the department.'

External hindrances

- people
  - who block, discourage or undermine us
  - whose perception of us is negative
  - who act with prejudice towards us
  - whose views of what is appropriate conflict with ours
- environmental factors including:
  - what is going on in our organisation, in our business or work arena, locally, nationally and internationally
  - the economy
  - competition on a personal, local or global level
  - technology
  - politics

Ingrid

'At school I had always wanted to be a sports teacher, but I was told "No black people are sports teachers". I thought what the teacher said must be right so I went to secretarial college and passed all the exams with flying colours. I got various temporary jobs and earned quite a lot of money.

'I started work as a secretary for a housing association and was then promoted to the position of fair rents assistant. Soon after, the manager left and his position was vacant for quite some time. I just got on with the work and didn't think anything about the fact I was doing the work of two. Two people had a go at doing the manager's job but they didn't last. Eventually someone said "Why don't you go for it?". I applied but was turned down. I was told it was because I didn't have the professional qualifications, but this had not been a criterion for selection. It suddenly dawned on me that I was being discriminated against in three areas – my colour, my age and my gender.

'I took the plunge and went into grievance, which I won. It was at that time I realised that I was capable of so much more and started to take my career really seriously. I changed organisations and went for some decent qualifications and training, which I believe has now paid off. The experience has taught me it's up to me to stand up for myself and ask for what I need. Unfortunately no one is going to do it for you.'

External helps

- people who support or encourage us, from whom we learn, who help practically with information or advice
- environmental factors, if we are alert to take-advantage of the opportunities they present
- chance or fortunate circumstances, but *not* luck!

*   *'I realised that by always saying I was lucky I was minimising the considerable efforts I had expended to make my own luck.'*
*   *'When my manager was on long-term sick leave her place was taken by another senior colleague who really encouraged me by drafting me onto an important working party, regularly asking for my opinion and suggesting that I apply for promotion – which I got outside the organisation. My career, which up to then I had felt was blocked, really took off.'*

EXERCISE –
HELPS AND HINDRANCES

*   Using the above lists as a guide, generate your own list of the things that have helped and hindered your career to date.
*   Think about how you can create the most from potential helps and minimise or avoid the hindrances.

UNDERSTANDING THE PRESENT

Focusing attention on the present and how we feel about it can facilitate the process of moving on in whatever directions we wish. Alternatively it can confirm that we are happy doing what we are, where we are, and make it easier to resist others' expectations and plans for us.

Accurate objective knowledge of the present and our experience of it is an important ingredient of empowerment. Analysing the current

59

situation and the extent to which it uses our gifts, satisfies our needs and allows expression to our key values can provide surprises or validate our feelings by grounding them in reason. An appreciation of what we need to cope and thrive in our working and personal lives and the relationship between the two can help in striving for home/work balance. This area is explored in Chapter 3.

Looking at all the aspects of your life it is useful to be clear about the following:

- How successful are you at present? By whose definition of success?
- Is there sufficient challenge for you right now?
- What opportunities are there for you to use your skills fully?
- Is there enough variety?
- Are you having fun?
- Is there enough new learning to interest you?
- Are you sufficiently supported in your work?

EXERCISE –
A PERFECT DAY

- Write a description of a perfect day for you. Allow your imagination free rein and include all the things in the day that you would really like if you could choose.
- Be as precise and detailed as you wish,

---

but include all aspects of the day, such
as where you are and with whom.
- Think about how the day begins and
  ends and the activities you are involved
  in throughout.

Identifying what to change

Assessing our satisfaction with the whole picture of our lives and the specific elements within
it can lead us to clarify what it is we wish to
work on. From there we can move to analyse the
potential choices.

Fiona

Throughout her working life Fiona worked hard at getting the
balance in her life that meant she spent enough time with her
family. With two children and with both partners having demand-
ing public sector managerial roles, they identified that childcare
caused them the greatest concern. Balancing all the elements was
a constant struggle, with unsatisfactory results for everyone. As
Fiona's career had progressed more rapidly than her husband's
and he was disgruntled with initiatives that affected his work,
they decided to make major changes. Her application for a senior
post was successful and he resigned to care for the children and
manage the home. After being in post for a year she made further
changes to the structure of her working life that enabled her to
work at home one morning a week and thus take her children to
school, and she and her husband made a weekly commitment
to go swimming together alone.

EXERCISE -
WHOLE LIFE PICTURE

• Draw a circle and then divide it into segments to represent the elements in your
  life. You might include paid work,
  family, domestic chores, travelling, a
  hobby, sport etc.

• Ask yourself:

  Overall what is the balance between the
  different segments like?
  How does it look in relation to how I
  would like it to look?
  Which segments are causing concern for
  me?

• For each segment that causes you concern, consider specifically:

  What am I satisfied and dissatisfied
  with?
  What do I keep moaning about?
  What do I want to change?
  What changes would improve the
  situation?

The job role

If it is the job role that we wish to change we
need to explore how we would prefer it to be and
consider:

• The job itself
  – Does the work itself interest us?

- Are our entrepreneurial or security needs met?
- Are we continuing to develop our skills and knowledge as appropriate for our needs?
- Are we able to operate at a level that is satisfying?
- The environment for the job
  - Is the environment the right one for us?
  - To what extent do we feel comfortable within the organisation's size?
  - How much time do we need to spend on the organisational issues?
- The working relationships
  - How much time do we need to devote to developing and nurturing them?
  - Are we a team player or do we prefer working alone?
  - Is there sufficient opportunity for individuality?

EXERCISE –
THE PERFECT JOB

- Write a description of the perfect job for you.

- Include:
  - the nature of the job tasks (you could refer back to your interests here)
  - the people contact: type and amount
  - where you work and the general environment
  - the skills you are using
  - the values that drive the work and the organisation

> – the hours and the package
> – how it fits into your career life line
> – the opportunities it would bring you

We need to bear in mind how important it is to act on the surface in ways that are congruent with our own values (as discussed in Chapter 1). This can be an arena for conflict; stress arises when organisational and personal values clash.

Managing personal change

Whether externally or self imposed, change often involves pushing back boundaries and can create significant initial discomfort. Our own perceived payoffs for not changing can keep us inactive – and justify our inactivity.

Loretta

Loretta decided it was easier not to take the professional qualification that she needed to get promoted. Her decision meant that she wouldn't have to study in her own time and manage the associated stress. The payoff was that she could convince herself that this was the only reason she was not progressing within the company and ignore the possible other reasons.

Recognising and tackling the payoffs whilst identifying the benefits can help us move forward.

Justine

In a rut with her job, Justine explored and listed the payoffs of not changing – either the job or the conditions she experienced. 'One is that I can keep whinging and blaming the job. I won't

64

have to put effort and energy into looking for a new one and can wait for things to change and then blame them when they don't. If I stay where I am, I won't experience rejection and have to deal with all those feelings. But at the end of the day changing means I have to confront some things about me and I would have to change the way I deal with people.

'I'd also have the potential for achieving what I want, and that seems a bit scary. But the benefits of change are very attractive. They include better job prospects and pay, improved work conditions and relationships, less of the hassle I'm getting from an organisation that makes ridiculous demands and a manager who seems to try to prevent me doing my job by his actions. Ultimately I'd have greater calmness and focus in my life and that's important.'

What helps us make the transition?

Change involves letting go of something old – an old way of behaving, for example – to allow

---

EXERCISE – PAYOFFS AND BENEFITS OF CHANGING

- If you have been considering areas of personal change, answer the following questions:

  What are the payoffs for carrying on exactly as I am?

  What are the benefits of change?

  Is what stops me changing internal or external to me?

  What would help me in the change process?

something new in to our life. For this transition to take effect we have to mourn the old way and go through a range of emotions from sadness to anger. In this process there will be a time when we are fumbling between the old and the new. We might not have the skills or knowledge to deal effectively with the new, but we have accepted that our old ways are redundant, inappropriate or need to change.

What will help us in transition is:

- accepting that change is inevitable in life and is difficult for everyone
- appreciating there will be different ways of seeing a situation and different ways of doing things and that no one way is completely right or completely wrong
- accepting that we will make mistakes and can bounce back and that perfection is unrealistic
- recognising that change is a process of small steps and transition stages where calculated risk is acceptable
- valuing what experience has taught us
- being clear about what is important to us – our values and priorities
- identifying sources of support and help

Tracey

Tracey is successfully self-employed as a public relations con-sultant. 'Looking back I realise that the transition to self-employment was relatively painless because the process had started five years ago. Without planning too much I had made a conscious decision to acquire the necessary skills and contacts. I realise the biggest thing that helped me was discovering that I am really unhappy working in a large corporation. At the time it seemed like a real problem, but in fact it helped me clarify what is important to me as an individual.'

Ciara

Ciara was working as a marketing executive for an international publication. For two years she was filled with dread before work every morning and she could not understand where the problem lay. She kept blaming her manager and the company. Finally she decided she had had enough and handed in her notice. 'I wanted to work abroad and have always had a flair for languages so I decided to train to teach English as a foreign language. It's the best decision I've ever made. I love the weather and lifestyle and bringing up my children in Spain. It's only now looking back that I can see I was in direct conflict with my values when I worked for the magazine.'

What is progress?

Amy

As a successful and gifted social worker, Amy was very clear that progress for her lay in being effective in her client contact roles and that this was at the centre of her work satisfaction. Intelligent, visionary and organised, she had to work hard at resisting the wishes of others in her organisation and family to push her towards a leadership position. Progress for her meant doing an excellent job as well as having a full life outside work, using her creative talents and spiritual commitment in a variety of contexts.

Understanding what progress means in our terms is a prerequisite for career development. This involves identifying past and present satisfaction and, through a process of elimination, selecting the significant features for the future. Trusting gut feelings about what is important and not minimising our intuition about what we really want is integral. Sometimes it is a feeling

67

that will drive us to greater understanding when the logical step is to stay put.

Liane

Liane was determined to change direction completely despite everyone telling her how successful she was, what a bright future she had and emphasising all the benefits of staying. However, a steady and secure local job in pleasant surroundings with congenial colleagues, opportunities for promotion and work she enjoyed, a good income and long holidays were not enough to keep her from making a career change. Listing the pros and cons of changing produced a clear logic to stay. The gut feeling that she was not really fulfilled and using her talents to the full was the spur to action. 'Knowing what you want is the hardest thing of all. Once that is clear the rest is relatively plain sailing. I needed to stick with the feelings, gather as much information as I could and then jump. Taking a risk for a situation that I hoped would be better proved to be the best, if the most difficult thing I did.'

EXERCISE – DECIDING WHAT TO CHANGE

- In your present role (including both paid work and the other areas of your life) consider:

   What aspects am I unhappy with?
   What aspects am I happy with?

- Identify what you need to change, considering:

   Is it the career progression?
   Is it the work setting?

> Is it the job role?
> Is it the balance of my work and per-
> sonal life?

PLANNING AHEAD

Focusing on aspirations

Planning ahead involves clarifying what it is we aspire to. Often we will have lost touch with the real dreams, or be too busy to believe they can be translated into reality. We might be actively pursuing someone else's dreams or plans, with little attention to our own.

It can be helpful to kick out the 'shoulds' and fun to explore the things we feel we ought not aspire to. Who told us that it was not OK to want to travel the world, give up paid work for the family or paint? Why do we believe that the treadmill is preferable, that everyone else must come first, that a woman's role is . . . ? Caught up in social assumptions or our own prior learning and perceptions, we will often accept the norms.

The satisfaction and joy of doing what we desire with our lives are well worth the time and struggle spent deciding what we do want.

Joan

'When I attended the Pepperell Development Course one of the questions that we were asked "What do I want to achieve before I die?" It really focused my mind. As a result I have climbed the Himalayas and driven a motorbike around the

69

United States and Australia. If the question had never been asked I don't know whether I would have fulfilled my ambitions.'

EXERCISE –
ASPIRATIONS

- If you want to pin-point your aspirations a bit more, try putting marks of 1 (very little) to 5 (a great deal) against the following possible goals in life. Then see in what order they come out.

LEADERSHIP
to become an influential leader; to organize and empower others to achieve community or organisational goals

---

EXPERTISE
To become an authority on a special subject; to persevere to reach a hoped-for expert level of skill and accomplishment

---

PRESTIGE
To become well-known; to obtain recognition, awards or high social status

---

SERVICE
To contribute to the satisfaction of others; to be helpful to others who need it

WEALTH
To earn a great deal of money;
to build up a large financial
estate

INDEPENDENCE
To have the opportunity for
freedom of thought and action

AFFECTION
To obtain and share
companionship and affection
through immediate family and
friends

SECURITY
To achieve a secure and stable
position in work and financial
situations

---

*SELF-REALISATION/SELF-
GROWTH*
To optimise personal development; to realise my full
creative and innovative
potential; to have a sense of
achievement

SPIRITUALITY
To dedicate myself totally to the
pursuit of ultimate values, ideals
and principles

PLEASURE
To enjoy life; to be happy and
content; to have the good things in
life

ADVENTURE
To have the opportunities for
exploration, risks, excitement

- Add any other things, not on the list, to which you aspire
  and rate them too.

- Having clarified your aspirations, consider to what extent
  you devote time and energy in their pursuit. You could
  check back to the **Whole Life Picture Exercise** to help you
  answer this.

- In addition, by reviewing your career path you can see what
  aspirations have driven you so far.

Goal setting

Goals are the hills we want to reach. They can be
definite outcomes – for example a new job, a committed relationship or more holidays – or they can
be vague – such as greater opportunities for using
our skills, working in an organisation that is
nearer to our values or being in a financial position
to retire in so many years. Sometimes they can
seem like a logical progression from our current
position and sometimes they are about wild
dreams. They can be related to opportunities – and
threats – within our department, organisation or –

industry or just spring from our personal position. The important thing is that they are expressions of desire.

To set goals we have to believe we have the power to determine our future and the self-worth to deserve it. It requires courage and commitment, qualities that will stand us in good stead when we take the steps to reach our goals. Goals are separate from actions and need to be clarified without too great a focus on how we will achieve them. The practicalities can stop us dreaming by directing our attention to the distance between the present and the future and the difficulties we anticipate on the journey.

The timescales for goal setting are completely variable. Some people's goals range from 25 years to one week or a month! Many of us experience resistance to looking into the future like this. One reason is that, having expressed our desires, we will be even more disappointed if we do not achieve them. Another is the sense that we will miss out on opportunities that come along if we are rigidly focused on the future.

It is vital to remember that being clear about where we are going does not preclude us from enjoying the route, exploring diversions, or indeed changing direction altogether. It is not an attempt to drive single-mindedly ahead without stopping to reassess progress or just to pause for fun. We will need to have our feet firmly on the ground so that we do not trip up in our determination to reach our goal nor miss out on the experiences along the way. In essence it involves knowing where we want to be so that we know which road to choose and can recognise it when we get there.

EXERCISE –
SETTING GOALS

- Write down some goals that you have set in the past, already worked towards and perhaps achieved, even if not consciously.

- What sort of timescales were you working in?

- Define for yourself some long-term goals, medium-term goals and short-term goals using your own preferred timescales.

- For each goal, list the advantages and disadvantages of achieving it.

- From this, decide which ones are really important to you.

- Taking each goal in turn, identify what you have done already to move you towards achieving it.

Turning goals into actions

Action planning is a tool to turn dreams into reality. It involves the setting of very specific and concrete steps which will take us steadily towards our goals. Commitment to achieving the actions can be maintained by structuring review periods into the plan, with personally relevant treats for actions achieved and opportunities to reschedule if they are not. If they are not, it is useful to clarify that the goal is still really desired; if it is, then identifying the obstacles to action – including any excuses! – will give further actions to overcome them.

At its best, action planning is a self-directed and self-driven empowerment technique. It should not seem like a straitjacket, though, that restricts the pursuit of other possibilities that may arise. By regularly looking back, thinking of the present and action planning for the future, the career development framework becomes a way of life.

Michaela

Michaela had almost completed her professional training, but felt she was at crisis point with her company. She worked for a large, blue chip conglomerate. The attitude prevailed that it was a privilege to work for them and 'you should be grateful that you are allowed to sign your own memos'. She was told that as the only woman in her position she was seen as an experiment. She had come to a point when she was ready to resign.

By working through her career and life line she realised she had a large reservoir of highly marketable skills and strengths. She realised that although she hated the job and the organisation she needed to bide her time for two reasons. First, she needed the company to sponsor her membership to her professional institution and, secondly, having the company on her CV would give her access to other blue chip organisations, even though she did not have much responsibility.

As soon as she was fully qualified and a member of her professional institute she left the organisation for a job she loves. She said she found that by taking stock through the career & life line she was not quite ready to move on. Taking responsibility helped her to be more strategic about her next move and clearer about what she needed to achieve. Ironically when she was going to leave her old company they offered promotion and extra money to persuade her to stay.

Action planning tips

* Take time to think
* Gather relevant information
* Find sources of personal support
* Get useful experience and qualifications
* Make contacts
* Start small and let it grow – avoid grand designs
* Think and act strategically

75

* Be realistic about timescales – do not expect overnight changes
* Accept the need for external help on occasions – to observe, to discuss or to provide formal training
* Be alive to opportunities afforded by the development process – there may be a chain reaction
* Be cautious – development cannot be forced on the unwilling
* Review your progress and set further actions
* Obtain feedback from others
* Actions should be SMART   S – specific
                                      M – measurable
                                      A – achievable
                                      R – relevant   (to the goal)
                                      T – timed

SUMMARY – CAREER LIFE PLANNING EXERCISE

* Identify what is important to you (you will have done some work on this if you completed the values and aspirations exercises).

* **Goals**
Draw up a list of things you hope to achieve. Let your imagination work here. Try not to censor yourself or impose blocks to your creativity – go with your dreams for the sake of the exercise. Later you can think about turning them into reality.
Explore the advantages and disavantages to you of achieving your goals and check they are still pertinent.

* **Timescales**
Divide your list into – long-term goals

    – medium-term goals

    – short-term goals

Use a timescale that makes sense to you – e.g. long-term might be 10 years, 5 years or 1 year – and then work backwards.

- **Priorities**

  Take a look at your goals. Check if they are important and that you really want to strive for them. Whilst doing this prioritise them into most important, second most important and so on.

- **Goals into actions**

  Think of the steps you could take to achieve these goals. Sometimes these may not be clear or may seem impossible, but creative thinking, discussion and help can often lead to breakthroughs.

- **Action planning**

  Now develop a detailed action plan to take steps towards the goals.

- **Helps and hindrances**

  or each of your actions ask yourself:

  – who or what could help me?

  – who or what could hinder me?

  Identify the further actions you can take to harness the helps and minimise the hindrances.

- **A proviso**

  Remember that career life planning is not rigid and inflexible. It is to give you direction in your career, not a detailed route. It is to help you generate clarity of purpose and vision and thus needs to be open to changes in you and to opportunities that occur. Keep your eyes on the hills, but do not be so caught up with where you are going that you fail to see what is happening around you and how that may help you on your journey.

3
POWERFUL STRESS

*At the worst, a house unkempt cannot be so
distressing as a life unlived.*
(Rose Macaulay)

THE IMPACT OF STRESS IN OUR LIVES

This chapter explores ways of taking responsibility for the impact of stress on our lives and making that impact more positively powerful. We cannot do this without a greater understanding of the tensions that create stress, and our personal reactions to them.

In our experience, people either lack practical ideas for managing their stress and time, or know very well what they need to do but do not do it, saying they have no time. The extent to which we are prepared to take constructive time for ourselves mirrors our seriousness about our own development.

> * 'I realised that I was no use to anyone else if I was exhausted all the time.'
> * 'Those extra busy times when I have neglected myself I have eventually suffered more. My back, which is my weak spot, gives out.'

* *'I used to say I hadn't got time for all these stress strategies. Now I take the view that I haven't got time not to.'*
* *'There's no mystique to stress management. It's all really common sense and you just have to do it.'*
* *'When I take time to think and plan, or even to just look objectively at a difficult situation, I come up with much better ideas for tackling it, rather than just diving in.'*
* *'At the end of the day, I realise it's my responsibility to look after myself and sort out my priorities.'*
* *'Booking in holidays and treats not only gives me something to look forward to, but balances out the frenetic pace of my working life.'*
* *'By taking up pottery I use a completely different type of energy in contrast to the rest of my life. I get totally absorbed and switch off from everything else.'*
* *'Building in time for me, outside of my roles as mother, partner, daughter, friend and manager was very difficult, to start. However, I think I'm now more effective at them all because I look after myself.'*

DIVIDED LOYALTIES

We may well experience a sense of being tugged in different directions by the contrasting aspects of our lives. Having to respond to the pull between opposites divides our loyalties, and we will often absorb the tension created between the opposing poles. Identifying what it is that tugs at us and thus directs or diverts our energy – in the process creating negative energy – is the first step.

These demands often represent pressing needs, and their presence can lead to feelings of guilt for not responding to all of them, confusion about what is really important and an experience of being fragmented. In addition, responding to the needs of many others puts us into a state of busy-ness. By always being on the go we run the risk of 'activity overload' and forgetting how to stop: human doings rather than human beings. A consequence can be burn-out and exhaustion and the eventual inability to complete any tasks and fulfil anyone's needs.

Hannah

With a young baby and promoted position at work Hannah found that any time for herself was a complete luxury. 'I am on the go all day at work and then usually have to attend meetings that run late. When I get home I spend time with my daughter and after cooking and eating get on with the rest of my work. I'm pulled between doing a good job at work and caring for my family because I want the best for them. The outcome is no time for me at all. I am wondering how long I can keep on like this but I feel guilty about taking time for me or asking my husband to do more – which he would do. I want him to have time for himself too. I think when I get to my next holiday I'll try to arrange a regular night out for me but right now I don't have time or the mental energy to think about it clearly.'

Deidre

Deidre's job involved travelling over 500 miles each week visiting clients and regional offices. 'I am away from home at least two or three nights a week. I know I couldn't do this job if I had a family. However I still want to have a social life, try to get in some exercise, see my parents who don't live too far away. It doesn't seem too much to ask, but by the time I've sorted out any paperwork over the weekend or in the evenings I'm absolutely shattered. I end up resenting my parents and friends for wanting to see me – at the same time I love the job. Why can't there be a middle ground so I can please everyone and myself?'

THE COST OF STRESS

Responding to the conflicting demands can create what we experience as stress. Implicit in this response is how we see the demands and whether we feel we can cope with them. Often we are able to do just that – but at some cost. The costs are often to the things we hold to be important, usually to ourselves: our health, our relationships, our friends and our leisure time, perhaps our career, our happiness and our satisfaction.

Marisa

Marisa works as a fundraiser for a charity. 'A lot of my work is done outside the normal 9–5 hours, in the evening and weekends. My partner is getting really annoyed and unsympathetic because sometimes it feels like the only time we see each other is if he comes along to an event. When I have a weekend free I just want to crash out; because his job is more routine he wants to party.'

HOW MUCH STRESS?

Just as some people are able to balance the elements in their lives easily, sail through tensions and seem less vulnerable to the unhealthy effects of stress, so some of us are more susceptible and experience discomfort in stress. Whereas some find many situations and experiences stressful, others thrive on pressure and actually create further stress for themselves.

Sometimes we compare ourselves unfavourably with others in terms of what we can take on. The great differences between us regarding the tensions we can comfortably live with stem from our individuality, with one factor being the extent to which we can keep an appropriate amount of ourselves separate.

In addition to individual variations, our personal needs for pressure and reactions to it will change over time; what we handled quite easily last week may this week seem too much, an easy challenge becoming insurmountable. What makes the difference is the range of stress strategies we deploy. Whilst we need to find an appropriate level of these for us, it is important to recognise that we will need to step these up in really hectic times – just when we think the time is not available to do them at all!

HEALTHY AND UNHEALTHY STRESS

It is often assumed that all stress is bad, and yet we will all have experienced the adrenalin surge which lifts our performance and help us meet a challenge. The excitement and healthy buzz of responding to appropriate demands is healthy stress.

Insufficient stress for our individual needs, in contrast, can over time dull our senses, dampen our spirits, muddle our sense of purpose and deaden our sense of self. It is important not to confuse understress with the opposing experience of overstress. The key is to separate activity and challenge. Some of us might feel that we are are often incredibly busy, yet insufficiently challenged. We are not developing, learning, growing and feeling stimulated in ways that meet our stress needs.

At the other end of the scale, overstress is most commonly experienced as overload, feeling that everything is too much and that we cannot cope or carry on. It is a response to too many pressures over time with insufficient supports. We need to monitor our reactions to identify when we are heading for a period of overload. The key is change and, whilst bodily reactions can provide one set of clues, thoughts, feelings and actions are also significant. For example, we could notice:

- eating or sleeping problems
- increased mood swings
- lowering of self-esteem
- changed or exaggerated behavioural tendencies
- negative or irrational thoughts
- depleted energy
- constant tiredness
- behaving in ways that create more pressure, e.g. drinking or smoking more, cancelling any regular exercise
- lowered resistance to illness
- irritability, procrastination, indecision

In order to manage overstress, we need to build up a repertoire of practical strategies.

PRACTICAL STRESS STRATEGIES

Ways of coping with the pressures include:

- identifying and anticipating the causes
- managing the demands on our time
- changing the way we see a situation
- preventing the build-up of excess pressure
- changing our response to the pressures
- taking care of ourselves so we can cope more effectively

IDENTIFYING THE SOURCES OF STRESS

Confronting the forces that pull us in different directions is a significant step towards managing our response.

By analysing the demands and identifying what it is that tugs at us we have the potential to tackle any underlying issues that disempower us.

> * *'I have three children. I want to be a good mum and get involved with after school-activities, but sometimes it feels too much with the job as well. I just about keep my head above water.'*
> * *I really want to have a baby, but my partner isn't interested. He's had kids from his first marriage. My career is successful, but it isn't everything.'*
> * *'When my little boy is really ill I take time off. I feel terrible and don't tell my*

> *employer, because I think it's really looked down on. In fact they don't even know I have a child.'*
>
> * *'Because I am single there is an expectation from my colleagues that I have more time than anyone else to work late and help out in emergencies. I want to be helpful but I resent the assumption that my life is not important.'*
>
> * *'My husband and I recently moved six miles away from my widowed mother. She still expects me to pop in and see her every night after work. I do it, but really resent it because it means I get home even later.'*

When our particular tensions are identified and perhaps discussed we may well experience a sense that we are failing because we should be able to cope. This 'macho' attitude, often rooted in unrealistic stereotypes and comparisons, is not helpful because

- it stops us taking stock and accepting where we are at present, which is vital for positive change, and
- it prevents us finding ways to handle things differently.

To manage stress and lead healthy lives it is important that we allow greater self-awareness to develop, and this takes time. To get this time we have to accept our limits realistically regarding our responses to all the 'pulls'. These limits should be based on a recognition of what is appropriate for us in our unique circumstances regardless of what other people do or are capable of.

EXERCISE –
IDENTIFY THE TUGS/PULLS

Identify the particular tensions in your life that draw you in different directions.

MANAGING THE DEMANDS ON OUR TIME

If we are not achieving all that we want from our time or if we feel guilty at being torn in different directions we need to develop methods for deciding which task or whose needs should be addressed at that moment. First, however, we need to make time for ourselves.

The importance of 'me time'

Women often undervalue their own needs as a result of upbringing and social expectations. Women who sacrifice all of their own time for others gradually lose belief in their entitlement to personal time. If we fail to keep parts of ourselves and our lives separate, which nothing and no-one will touch, we erode our sense of well-being, have a confused sense of what is important and difficulties in prioritising. It is therefore essential to devote time to maintaining and developing the bits of us that are entirely independent of others, separate from the roles we play in relation to others, such as mother, wife, partner, employee, friend.

Teresa

'After my marriage broke up, I worked really hard to provide a good home for my children, I was trying to bring them up well and prove to my employer that I could cope with the change. In the end I was taken really ill and my doctor insisted that I have a half hour every day to do nothing – away from the kids. It was so difficult to begin with. I started off reading magazines; I painted my nails, and listened to the radio, then music. Finally I learnt to really enjoy this time for me doing nothing much.

'During the first few weeks the kids would knock on the door. Now they have learnt it's my private time and only come in during a real crisis – which has only happened once. They have also learnt to have their time too . . .'

Essentially, 'me time' is time spent looking after ourselves. It enables us to pay attention to the needs of our inner self rather than focusing on responding to the stimulus of outside. Often of course we keep ourselves very busy so that there is no time to look at the uncomfortable things we would rather avoid – like what is important, what we want, or indeed how we feel about our lives. The result is that we disempower ourselves.

'Me time' makes priority space for personal rejuvenation. Developing inner strength enables us to respond with flexibility to the variety of opposing demands and their tensions without losing touch with the real core self. This inner strength allows clarity of focus so we can make decisions with ease from a strong plan of priorities and values, and this clarity will itself fuel direction and vision.

EXERCISE –
TAKE REGULAR ME TIME

- Plan to start by taking at least 10 minutes a day of time that is just for you.
- If you are unused to having time for yourself, you might find it difficult to get started. The key is not to fill it with lots of activity, just think of a few things you might like to do – in time it will get easier.
- The objective is to create some space to think or just to be.

Determining our own priorities

In order to define tasks in terms of priority we need to consider the person or people to whom it is a priority. Clearly some tasks will be a higher priority to others than they are to us, and in some circumstances we will want to respond to that, our significant relationship with them making it a priority for us.

- *   attending the children's sports day
- *   spending regular time with my family
- *   cleaning and tidying up the flat
- *   helping a colleague prepare for an interview
- *   taking my mother to hospital

Sometimes we have absorbed a sense of priorities along with our gender and carry around messages telling us what we 'should' be devoting attention to because we are women. Women report these 'shoulds' becoming louder at times of unhealthy stress when it is easier to stop thinking and instead conform to old and obsolete notions based on others' expectations of what is important.

---

* *dropping my work demands to listen to someone else's problems*
* *drying the dishes*
* *ensuring that everyone's clothes are ironed so they know I'm a good homemaker*
* *cancelling my social engagements when my partner wants to do something else*
* *making complicated birthday cakes for my family*

As a result of our conditioning and because of concern for our relationships, we run the risk of considering every one else's priorities to the exclusion of our own. If we continue to do this we may never identify what is important for us.

---

* *quality conversations with my partner*
* *getting my legs waxed*
* *watching soaps on television*
* *booking a holiday*
* *studying for my exams*
* *going for a swim*

EXERCISE –
PRIORITIES

This exercise is to review the priority source of the tasks you regularly do. It can help you to see more clearly where your attention is going and check that it is appropriate.

It would be useful to complete it at a busy time or just before a weekend when you feel that you have lots to do.

- Quickly make a 'to do' list of all the tasks you have in mind that have to be completed today or over the next few days.

- Now make two columns denoting whether the task is a priority mainly to someone else or to you and decide in which column each task should go. If the priority is both to another and also to you, draw arrows horizontally between the columns to show the link between your own and others' priorities.

Priority to another	Priority to me

- Consider if there is any conflict between those priorities that are only to others and those that are only to you. Would discussion between relevant parties about them help?
- Are there any priorities in the first column that you could cross off your 'to do' list?
- If there are no items in the second column, think about what you would really like to put there.
- Now go back and put the items on your 'to do' list in priority order.
- Are there any learning points for you from this exercise about the source of your priorities?

Sharing the domestic load

For many of us our self-esteem is connected with the success of our roles as mother, home-maker, wife or partner. It may be that we perceive some of our personal power as coming from running the home, but if we are also working outside the home we can find the 'double shift' leaves us with no energy left for ourselves. Some women refuse to accept that home running is their job, others are happy to accept that it is. However, the reality is that in most households women take on more of either the routine tasks or their organisation.

As empowerment implies making choices, for many women this can mean changing the pattern of domestic maintenance and initially enlisting support with specific tasks.For some women it involves challenging any beliefs – held by themselves or significant others – that the home is their responsibility. For this to work we also have to relinquish our monopoly on what is right in the home and share the power.

Danuta

'I realise it was no good imposing my standards on my partner about the way I wanted the sheets to be changed. He would say "I'm going to do it my way or not at all". I've learnt that it's not that important. It is something I've got to let go of – at least the job is done. I do draw the line though at him using the brillo pad on the enamel bath!'

Sharing either the power or the task incorporates other family members into the running of the home. By relinquishing some of the routine chores, we are freeing up our time to relax, think, take stock and conserve energy so we can be more effective in what we do both in and out of our relationships. We are also preparing children with the skills they need for adulthood and independence as well as sharing the responsibility of maintaining the home with our partner.

Suzanna

Suzanna is a single parent with a full-time job. 'Since the breakup of my marriage I have over-compensated in many respects by taking on everything in the house. One of the biggest chores was the ironing for three of us.

'I realised my teenagers could be doing their own ironing so I took them through their paces despite the resistance. I finally told them it would be up to them to do their ironing. The conflict was terrible, they wouldn't do it and went out with crumpled clothes. I felt awful and thought everyone would think what a terrible mother I was. Sometimes I ended up doing it for them and of course that made it worse as they knew they could manipulate me. I had to decide what was more important in the long term – them ironing for themselves or me seeing them in pressed clothes now. I believe it is their responsibility and if they look a mess that's tough.'

To share the load we need to think through how we are going to approach members of the family to help us. In general it is helpful to consider how best to tackle this based on knowledge of the individuals concerned. The following principles can help.

- Raise the issue of sharing particular tasks before they need to be done.
- Specify exactly what the tasks are and what they entail, allowing the person to do them their way.

- If the individual has never done the job before, show them how you do it and ask them how they might approach it. Bear in mind there may be wrong ways of doing something, but there is no absolute right way.
- Give the person permission to make mistakes and learn from them. The way we handle the mistake will influence their attitude to the task. If we are sarcastic or lose our temper they will certainly not feel so inclined to continue.
- Recognise and, if appropriate, reward effort.
- Think if there is other help that you can draw on, and what tasks you can drop that are actually not that important.

Surinda

'I found everytime I asked my husband or children to help me when I was cleaning the house they would say no. I would get angry and carry on doing it. I found that if I was over-emotional or nearing the last straw because I was tired they wouldn't take me seriously or they would do it out of guilt. When I ask them to help whem I'm calm it has a much more positive outcome.'

Dealing with guilt

Many of the women who have attended our courses report that guilt is a great pressure. Guilt is a learnt rather than an innate emotion. It is a useful barometer of feelings about behaviour that is contary to our beliefs and values. Guilt may have been the means by which our parents, teachers and other significant adults corrected our behaviour when we did not fulfil their expectations, which is why it is so powerful.

If our self-worth comes from meeting and taking care of the needs of others, it can be hard to stand up for our own needs. In fact, if there is a conflict between what we need and the other person's needs many women automatically put the other person first. Whilst not denying the value of concern for others, when this becomes a trend that stops us thinking of ourselves at all it can cumulatively cause extremely unhealthy stress. One result of such behaviour can be the 'martyr or victim' syndrome, which in turn may create guilt in others, so perpetuating the cycle of stress and resentment.

Lisa

'When I had my first baby she was quite ill. I desperately wanted to be a good mother and wife. I thought deep down inside that womanhood has finally arrived and yet I felt I couldn't cope with all of the responsibility. I didn't get much help because I thought I shouldn't ask for it. If I did I was failing in some way. Other women had coped, therefore so should I. Being at home full-time I felt the house should be clean and my husband should come home to a cooked meal, and with the feeds and generally looking after the baby. I was shattered all the time. It was only when I got extremely depressed that I got some help and realised I didn't have to do it all by myself.'

Acknowledging that we are entitled to time, space, support, reward and recognition can be uncomfortable for many women. It can be perceived as being selfish. The reality is that a certain 'selfishness' is essential. This does not mean walking all over everyone else; it does mean not encouraging others to walk all over us. Others will not necessarily speak up for us and if we are to become really empowered it is our responsibility to do it for ourselves.

Treating ourselves with respect is, in fact, treating ourselves as we would treat someone else we respected. It is a recognition that we deserve respect.

---

*   'I always find it difficult to refuse my sister when she wants to borrow my car. It is difficult for her to drop the children off and get to work, but I find I am having difficulty getting to work myself without it. The trouble is that now she has got used to having it once a week, if I say no I feel guilty.'

*   'Because I work long hours I make a point of separating my social and work lives very definitely. When a client's wife asked me to join them at the theatre I found it very hard to refuse, particularly as I did not want to jeopardise the contract.'

*   'As an experienced member of my team I get several demands and requests to help other people. At times it really has got out of hand. However I made a decision that I would take on only supporting activities that would enhance and help me to do my job more effectively – before I could help others.'

*   'I found that as soon as people discovered I was a trained counsellor they would open up and tell me their problems. It is not my responsibility to sort them out and just because I have the skill it does not mean I always have to listen to them. In the long term I think if people really want to sort a serious problem out they will get formal help. If my close friends and colleagues need help I will do what I can.'

Paying more attention to others' expectations of us rather than to our own can fuel guilt. Knowing what is acceptable, reasonable and realistic strengthens us against attacks to our self and the choices we make. This theme is pursued more in Chapters 4 and 5.

Clarifying the most important things

It is disempowering to be working at fundamental cross-purposes to others and thus a positive act is to clarify perceptions of what is important with other people who have an impact on our life and on whose lives we impact. Any difference in viewpoint can easily cloud our own vision and make life fraught or muddled.

Vashti

'The perceived view in my organisation is that if you want to get on and get things done you work long hours. Before my children I was happy to go along with it. However after my first child I realised it was totally unrealistic.

'I negotiated to work from 7am until 4pm. At first I received

quite a few snide comments so I checked out with senior managers whether this was causing a serious problem for them. I also pointed out that I did not waste any time while I was at work and that as a foreign exchange dealer many of our clients found it useful for me to be in so early while they were finishing off their day. The senior managers reaffirmed my position and people have now stopped.'

Penny

'The busiest day for me is our annual open day as I am totally responsible for managing this whole school event. Preparations take weeks and on the day there are always problems to deal with. There are exhibitions and displays, prospective students and parents are there and it is an opportunity to present the school to our community. I had worked really hard, it had gone superbly and I had stayed late to congratulate my team. When I got home all my husband could say was why was his dinner not ready.'

EXERCISE–
MOST IMPORTANT THINGS

- Answer the following questions, either by jotting down your answers or by discussing them with a friend
  What are the three most important things in your life right now?
    (NB. If 3 is inappropriate make it 2–5 most important things.)
  To what extent does the time you spend on them reflect their importance?
  What conclusions can you draw from your responses?
  Can you discuss this with significant people in your life?

Defining statements of purpose

Women generally have many different aspects to their lives and the challenge is maintaining them all in ways that are satisfying and effective.It is a myth to believe we can have everything at the same time. Doing something well usually means a trade-off – letting go of something else for a short period. Our energy is much greater and we are more effective if we are clear, not only about what we want, but also about what we need to put on the back-burner.

As we have considered, others' priorities can crowd out our own, drawing us into activity when we are too busy to reflect on whether it is appropriate or necessary or if our time would be better spent elsewhere. Being clear about the reasons for doing something helps us decide if it is a priority. Because activity itself absorbs our attention, we need a quick decision-making method that helps determine where we put our energies and confirms our decisions without guilt.

Charlotte

'Our organisation went through a downsizing programme. We had to make several thousand people redundant. It was decided the kindest way was to provide them with the support and package they needed, but to do it as quickly as possible. It meant that for six months my team and I worked incredibly long hours – evenings and weekends. I felt at the time my purpose was to ensure that people left with dignity and a decent package. There was a short-term cost to my family life. However, if I didn't do it I felt I would have let my team and the people I was helping down. I was clear in my own mind it would be for six months only.'

Betty

Betty was working for her Open University exams with a full-time job. She was also involved in her church's venture scout unit as a leader. 'I realised I couldn't do it all, something had to go. Although I enjoy being a venture scout leader enormously I had to let it go for a year. I told my boss how I was struggling and she agreed to give me a week's study leave in addition to my holiday entitlement.'

Clear statements of purpose that relate to different areas of our life facilitate the quick and the more considered choices, and help us defend them to ourselves and others, if necessary. They also help us differentiate between the opposing forces that can stress us but also make our lives exciting and fulfilling.

---

* *'My work role is to help people learn.'*
* *'At work my purpose is to maximise profits in my department.'*
* *'I want to ensure that my children have a happy and stimulating childhood.'*
* *'This year I am learning as much as I can about the new company I've joined.'*
* *'My purpose is to ensure the organisation is profitable and to build up morale again.'*
* *'My purpose this year is to build up my social life.'*

Statements of purpose are short (ideally no more than fifteen words) so they are easily memorised.Generally we will have a number of them to accommodate all the life roles. Having statements of purpose for our work role, including ones that encapsulate our time-related targets, will help to focus our energies in the workplace. They can also be set for our personal goals in any time period, for example defining our purpose for each day or for a meeting.

It is essential to have a statement of purpose for ourselves independent of our other roles, although this can be the hardest to define. It may change over time and adding in different ones for time periods (each year for example) can guide our development.

---

*   *'For the next six months my focus is to pass my exams.'*
*   *'This year I'm really aiming to have greater balance so I am not going to work such long hours.'*
*   *'After my divorce my purpose is to provide a secure home for my children.'*
*   *'This year I am saving for a long trip abroad.'*

EXERCISE –
STATEMENTS OF PURPOSE

*   For the different aspects of your life write brief statements of purpose.
*   Include a general one for any paid work role you have and a specific one for your current major concern at work.
*   Work towards defining your overall purpose in your whole life.

When confronted with lots to do or hard choices we can then consider which tasks relate to which purpose and make a more rational choice. We can also separate out the dimensions of our lives and thus switch mode more easily. To identify the order in which to tackle different demands we need to be clear about which purpose is top priority in our lives and about the general order the rest fall into.

Coping with large or long-term tasks

Other factors influencing the choices we make about tasks are the length of time they will take, the apparent benefit timescale and the size of the task.

Tasks that are quick to do and have an immediate effect or benefit can seem the more manageable. The obvious and immediate benefit attracts us and diverts attention from the bigger picture. An outcome that will not be experienced until some future time can, although of major benefit, seem small scale in comparison.

Because something is easy and urgent and has instant impact it tends to get done. Something that is less urgent and that will have impact at some future time will often be put to the bottom of the pile. In work-related activities, the longer-term, more complex tasks tend to be strategic initiatives, whilst the immediate demands are related to operational issues. This focus can be applied to both organisational and personal matters. Operational maintenance is clearly important, but if that is where all our attention and energy go we will not be seeing the future or tackling the larger and more complex activities that can be really important.

101

Chris

Chris is a finance officer with a local authority. 'For a long time the departments in the authority have been getting by on an old procedure manual that covers the accounting and computer system. The computer system has been upgraded, but no one wanted to take responsibility for upgrading the procedures. It meant we were constantly getting phone calls about problems or were having to return work to be done again. The staff involved had received some training but they couldn't remember everything.

'I could see that someone would have to update the procedures. Everyone would benefit as the finance department wouldn't have to deal with so many queries, the departments would have a quick easy reference guide and I would benefit in terms of the experience and achievement. It was hard not to let the more routine tasks take over. However, by blocking out the time I managed and it has proved really worthwhile. I regularly update the manual and have also developed my training skills.'

EXERCISE – BITE SIZE CHUNKS

- For any large task that you have been putting off tackling, make a start by breaking it into easily manageable mini-tasks.

- Set a date to deal with the first one.

- When that is done, reschedule your next step.

- Make this a regular practice.

A task that is huge can be completely off-putting. However, by breaking the task into chunks that are easily manageable – bite-sized in fact – we reduce each element to the status of a quick and achievable activity, and so can progress the task without having to deal with its enormity.

CHANGING THE WAY WE SEE A SITUATION

How we think and feel about ourselves and a particular situation will play an important part in our experience of and response to stress, although we may not consciously be aware of this. Other factors such as previous learning, current and recent events in our lives and the stress strategies we deploy – our unique combination of circumstances – will also play their part in how we handle a situation.

Our reactions to stressful situations can in themselves create more tension. By not asking for help we overload ourselves. By taking on others' views about what we should do or be and not following our own instincts there is danger that we act in ways that contradict our beliefs and possibly damage ourselves. The ways we view situations can also generate stress or increase our ability to handle it.

Maxine

Maxine was promoted to the position of account manager in her public relations firm. 'The promotion was given to me because of some important business I had handled. The problem I seemed to have was that I was given new responsibilities in addition to my old job. I wasn't coping at all well – I was working late and at weekends. I seemed to start projects off, but never finish them satisfactorily. I decided to write a memo to my boss.

103

'I told her that I wasn't coping at all well and listed all the areas of my job, which were quite considerable I showed the memo to a good friend and colleague, who also knows my boss. She pointed out that I sounded like a real victim and that it wouldn't wear very well with her. She went through the memo with me line by line and pointed out things I could delegate. She suggested that if after a month nothing had improved I send another memo, but slant it along the lines of "I really would like to make a more useful contribution to the business .. .". I waited a month and things had improved slightly, but not sufficiently, so I sent the new productive, positive memo. My boss gave me a sympathetic hearing and my work was redistributed so I could do a more effective job.'

Changing the way we see a situation is one strategy for managing stress and a good place to start is by looking at the expectations we have for ourselves. Self-imposed demands – the most insidious of pressures – can be at the root of the tension we experience. They can either overload or limit us. The standards we set for ourselves as we try to emulate 'superwoman' stop us doing the other things that are actually more important.

> * *'I thought I should be the perfect caring mother.'*
> * *'I felt that as a wife I should always put my husband's career first, regardless of circumstances.'*
> * *'I thought they would recognise my hard work and that would be the basis of my promotion.'*
> * *'I thought it was important to be liked by everyone.'*

> *   *'I thought I should cope with getting married, moving to another part of the country and a new job.'*
> *   *'I thought the quality of my dinner parties represented how much I valued my friends.'*

Unrealistic expectations derive from 'oughts' and 'shoulds' learnt during our lives. They lead to the perfection problem – striving for standards we will never attain. We have to challenge them for healthy stress. This involves setting realistic limits for our self-expectations. It also requires us to acknowledge that our energy is infinite only if it is replenished. We therefore have to create some boundaries that allow us to recharge our energies. For example, they can determine how many evenings we will work late or what is reasonable in terms of extra responsibilities, and confirm the times we want to spend doing other things.

> *   *'I make it a point to leave work on time at least twice a week.'*
> *   *'As a rule I never take work home at weekends.'*
> *   *'In general I attend only the parts of meetings that are pertinent to my area.'*
> *   *'If I have to cancel my exercise class I make a point of getting to another one that week.'*

> *   'If I take on new work responsibilities I aim to find something I can let go of by delegation.'
> *   'I will not entertain more than once a month.'

EXERCISE –
CHALLENGING UNREALISTIC EXPECTATIONS

•   Ask yourself the following questions:
What expectations do I have of myself? of others?
What beliefs do I have to challenge if I want to set realistic limits for myself?
What practical steps can I take to stop myself overloading?

PREVENTING THE BUILD-UP OF PRESSURE

Stressful situations often build up gradually. By the time we notice, it is much harder to take practical steps to change the situation as we will already be suffering the negative effects of stress and not thinking clearly.

It is vital that we take action to tackle pressures before they overwhelm us. This involves being alert to the pressures in all dimensions of our lives and taking steps to reduce them when we can or to plan for them when we have no choice. Particularly busy times might include any combinations of the following:

- Christmas
- end of term
- a busy time at work
- organising a family party
- taking exams
- completing a major project
- children changing schools or taking exams
- moving house
- partner's promotion or job change
- our promotion or job change

It is important to continue with the stress strategies at busy times. Even though they can seem like a low priority, they are in fact crucial as they strengthen us to cope. Appreciating the impossibility of keeping on relentlessly without breaks also helps us to resist the desire to keep on going. In addition we need to try to jettison some of the inessential activities to create space.

Asking for what we want can be difficult and something we avoid. Asking for help or support – and accepting it – is a strategy that confronts the fact that we are not perfect. Some find it more challenging to accept their limitations and ask for help than to struggle on. It is often easier to do this when the demands are obvious, for example periods of illness or when there is a bereavement or a new baby in the family. It is important to recognise that asking for help is an option in managing stress and to try to do it before times are really hard. We would be willing to help our friends and family, so we need to be willing to accept help.

The practical actions we could take to help reduce the pressures are enhanced if we become more assertive (which is explored in Chapters 5 & 6). This might include, for example:

- saying 'no'
- seeking more information
- clarifying others' expectations and maybe challenging them
- checking assumptions

EXERCISE –
TACKLING THE PRESSURES

- List five or six important pressures in your life.

- Taking each one individually, ask yourself:
  Can I change the situation in any way?
  If I can, what action could I take?
  If I cannot change the situation, can I influence it in some way?
  If I can, how and what action could I take?

CHANGING THE RESPONSE

When there is no action we can take, the only alternative is to learn to let the pressures go. This of course is easy in theory and hard in practice. However, if the alternative is to worry either at or about an issue with no possible benefit or practical outcome, then letting go has much to recommend it and is worth striving for. This can involve:

- refusing to go over it in our mind
- learning not to care so much
- increasing our strategies for caring for ourselves
- talking it through with someone to get it in perspective
- asking ourselves why are we hanging on to it.

Monique

Monique agreed that her mother-in-law could come and live with the family. 'The first few weeks weren't too bad, but as she gradually settled in she started to pick holes in the way I ran the house. To begin with I fumed and felt I couldn't say anything. Finally I lost my temper and we had a terrible row. She accused me of not wanting her to live with us. At the time she had a point.

'I realised I was in a no win situation. I was never going to change her and if I kept reacting I was playing into her hands and causing myself a lot of distress.Over a period of time I've learnt to let go. It's not easy all the time, especially if I'm tired, but most of the time I recognise the fact she doesn't have a lot to occupy herself. I've also asked her to help out more.'

TAKING CARE OF OURSELVES SO WE CAN COPE

In order to cope more effectively we need to make time for ourselves. Taking care of ourselves is an area of frequent neglect for women, who often do not even think of it. Supporting ourselves can seem inappropriate or unnecessary if we believe that someone else should take this role. Do we appreciate the bunch of flowers we buy for ourselves as much as that bought by another – or do we buy it at all?

Personal power and good self-esteem are built

109

up when we treat ourselves well and believe that we deserve to be treated well. The only person who can ensure this is us.

Emily

'As a little girl, a student nurse and then in personnel my self-esteem has always come from looking after the needs of others. The truth is I really enjoy being with people, so consequently all my social activities are also geared to helping my local community. I know I'm not a bottomless pit and yet I find it difficult to stop and say "no". When I have tried it's been because I'm ill or totally exhausted.'

It can be difficult to break a pattern of putting the needs of others before our own, but it is absolutely essential if we are to reclaim our personal power.

Putting ourselves at the centre requires that we devote energies in three activity focus areas: physical, inner self and social.

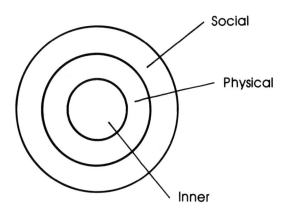

Looking after your physical self

The physiological changes of the automatic stress response are positive in that they prepare us for heightened activity and equip us to cope with the demands. However, physical equilibrium is not immediately restored and muscular tension – identified by headaches, shoulder or back pain – can signal that we have been experiencing a period of high pressure. Constant exposure to stressful situations, without activity to facilitate the return to balance, can leave us feeling exhausted. Because the body's continued response to too many demands creates further physical changes, overstress has been linked to illnesses affecting those organs or functions that adapt – the heart, skin, liver, blood, digestive system, sex organs and immune system.

Managing stress effectively is therefore helped by the best general state of health we can attain. This also gives us a strong base from which to move towards happiness and fulfilment while meeting all the demands on us – others' needs, those of our job and our own. Yet activities to develop or maintain fitness and health tend to come low on the priority list. Expecting that we will just be able to go on and on with no personal maintenance is unrealistic. We will all appreciate the protective sense behind the regular car service and routine checks to avoid the risk of motorway breakdown; similarly devoting routine time to maintaining ourself could ensure that we too start in the morning. We have a primary responsibility to look after ourselves, as well as others and a right to space and time for the aspects of life that give us pleasure.

EXERCISES –
FOR GOOD HEALTH AND ENERGY

The following suggestions are designed not to increase the pressure, but to help you to handle it. Aim to take one action from each section.

Exercise

When under pressure, often the last thing we feel like doing is making the effort to exercise, yet it *will* help build stress fitness.

Aim to take regular exercise. Start gradually and build it up. It is better to do 5 minutes than none at all, but ideally we should at minimum exercise for 20 minutes, three times a week.

Choose something you will enjoy and that fits into your life with as much ease as possible. If you think this will be hard, arrange to do it with a friend or make a financial commitment to keep you motivated. Gentle exercise – swimming or walking – is fine as well as aerobic exercise but if embarking on a vigorous programme do check with your doctor first.

Other ideas:

- buy an exercise bike, rowing machine or rebounder – and use it!
- choose from the huge selection of exercise videos
- join the local leisure centre or a sports club

- go to a dance class
- use a local gym
- walk or run every day

Relaxation
Take time to learn to relax physically and make it a part of your routine.

- use the relaxation tapes which are increasingly available in good bookshops
  - try yoga or the Alexander technique to learn to let the muscular tension dissolve
- take a long relaxing bath with your favourite bath oil
- use a sauna or steam room (not if you have high blood pressure or are pregnant)
- book a massage
- develop your own best ways to help you wind down

Diet
Consider your diet and find one that suits your body.

- maximise on fresh fruit and vegetables
- ensure that you get the minerals and vitamins you need
- reduce coffee, tea and cola drinks that contain caffeine
- at times of high pressure watch that you do not increase your junk food intake or miss out on meals, aiming for at least one well-balanced meal a day

- Stephanie Mills of the Academy of Systematic Kinesiology recommends drinking at least eight glasses of water daily – more at times of high pressure – and taking a Vitamin B complex supplement for stress protection
- reduce alcohol intake

Sleep

All of us have a different requirement for sleep. Stress occurs if we do not have enough over a period of time. There are several practical things we can do if we experience sleep problems, which include:

- switch off from work at least two hours before you put your head on the pillow
- do not fight insomnia –the worst thing you can do is to get worked up
- if you have a head racing with thoughts write down everything you are thinking – getting it down on paper can help to get it in perspective
- ask yourself, 'Can I honestly do anything practical about the situation at 2.00 in the morning?'
- listen to your breathing and then tense and relax each part of your body, starting from your toes
- read a trashy novel
- have a hot drink, watch the television or do the ironing

If the condition persists, you may need to see your doctor or talk through what is going on with a good friend or a counsellor until the problem is resolved.

If you are going through a traumatic period such as divorce, bereavement, redundancy, it could be natural for you not to sleep. The most helpful thing you can do for yourself is to acknowledge what is going on in your life and talk about how you are feeling. Sometimes acceptance is the only way forward.

Do not forget your inner self

Although distracting the mind with physical activities helps with stress, intellectual pursuits that satisfy and absorb the mind beyond the immediate demands are also important. Just as physical exercise helps to recharge our physical batteries so time to BE helps to revive our inner self by the very act of allowing us to explore it.

Often we are too occupied to get back in touch with our feelings, beliefs and spiritual self. Using 'me time' to make space for quietness facilitates the process.

Expressing feelings in a safe place where we will be listened to and supported should not be a luxury, although it might seem so if we are more used to hearing others. Putting things into a personally relevant perspective and having some sense of meaning that drives us is important, as is keeping interested in things for the sheer joy of them and allowing the mind to be stretched and challenged.

EXERCISE –
NOURISH YOUR INNER SELF

- Incorporate one or more of the following into your routine:
  - make quiet time for yourself every day
  - talk about how you are feeling either close to or away from the issue
  - clarify your sense of what is important in life
  - learn to meditate
  - stop over-scheduling and leave time to be
  - learn something new for fun
  - explore your spiritual beliefs
  - explore complementary therapies

Encourage your social self

Awareness of our needs for company and fun is the first step towards ensuring that they are given outlets. Engaging in leisure activities with others as part of a group could also include activities with the family, providing they are not just focused on what everyone else wants.

EXERCISE – SOCIALISE

Select from these suggestions:
- join a club or evening class
- make regular time for friends whose company you enjoy
- take time to do something just for the fun of it

> • do not neglect your irresponsible self –
> sometimes it is good to rely on others to
> take the lead and not feel responsible for
> anything or anybody

WE HAVE ONLY ONE LIFE – ARE YOU IN CHARGE?

Empowerment is possible only if we manage our stress, rather than let it manage us. Achieving an appropriate balance between the different parts of our lives requires regular readjustment – balance is not static. For enjoyment, fulfilled potential and effectiveness we will need to shift our attention from time to time to encompass the different dimensions of our experience, ensuring that we make the most of all that life has to offer.

To maintain our equilibrium we must recognise the prospect of tensions, for example between our personal development and the maintenance of our present life, between time for ourself and success in the present job role, and use suitable stress strategies in varying quantities to meet our particular needs at that specific moment. Not only can they boost our energies, they may also afford us enjoyment in themselves.

Nigella

Nigella was desperately unhappy in her job and recognised that until she had completed her professional exams she would not be in a position to leave. Because she did not have a partner she had difficulty in achieving a healthy balance in her life and 117 *let work dominate. After taking stock she decided she would focus more on her personal life.*

Over a period of time she built in some valuable stress strategies. She invested in a rebounder, which she used for 10 minutes every morning to give her energy. She also took up a regular painting class and rekindled her interest in music. The greatest benefit was getting the job in perspective by placing less importance on it until she found a new one. Although she now has a new job she still maintains these activities, which give her a range of ways to counter its pressures and thus enable her to be effective at her job. But she finds they are fun too.

SUMMARY –
PRACTICAL TIPS

* Recognise that stress is an issue to be taken seriously
* Take action to tackle your pressures and be alert to their build-up
* Develop your own stress strategies
* Take regular 'me time'
* Plan for particularly high-pressure periods by increasing your stress strategies
* Challenge self-imposed pressures and unrealistic expectations
* Appreciate the impossibility of keeping on unrelentingly without breaks and recognise the need to reduce the pressures from time to time
* Learn to let some things go
* Value your time as well as your needs
* Do all this because you deserve it

PART II

DEVELOPING PERSONAL POWER

4
DEVELOPING INNER PERSONAL POWER

'No-one can make you feel inferior without your consent'
Eleanor Roosevelt

Personal power is determined by whether what we achieve is what we actually want and by the actions we take to help ourselves in the process. It cannot be measured by whether we have a successful career or by external trappings. Working on this chapter we have been aware of the negative mental habits, personal self-doubt and challenges to our self-esteem we have experienced. However, we have worked at practising all the tips we recommend – and achieved our goals!

WHAT IS PERSONAL POWER?

Our inner personal power is our positive inner sense of ourselves. It significantly affects how we experience and deal with the external environment. Thus it influences our quality of life, our career and our relationships.

Why is this such an important issue? Because our inner world filters our perceptions and underpins our interactions with our external world, personal power is a factor in:

- how good we feel about ourselves
- our ability to bounce back from setbacks
- our confidence to make and exercise choices
- the extent to which we are able to take risks
- our capacity to develop our potential – in all areas of our lives
- our relationships and communications with others

Positive personal power is not the prerogative of a few lucky people; anyone can develop it and learn to maintain it. Using our personal power does not necessitate disempowering others; instead we can use it to help others' power to flourish. We will find that the more we allow others power the more we have.

---

* 'Personal power allows me to exercise more choices in the way I live my life.'
* 'Personal power is about me feeling good about myself, regardless of my problems.'
* 'My personal power grows every time I take risks – and stop worrying about failing.'
* 'I enjoy my personal power when I do things for myself.'
* 'I feel more personally powerful when I help someone because I want to, not because I have to – and I don't tell anyone about it.'

> * 'My personal power grows when members of my team achieve their goals, because they are talented, they work hard and they use their initiative.'
> * I fell in love when I was 15 and woke up when I was 40. My personal power blossomed when I realised I am not an extension of my husband. I am a person in my own right.'

In this chapter we explore the components of inner personal power, including its links with self-esteem and self-confidence, and suggest strategies for developing and exercising it. Our personal power evolves out of three interconnected factors:

- our self-perception
- our behaviour
- other people's perception of us

In simple terms, how we view ourselves determines our habits of behaving with others which creates their view of us and influences their behaviour towards us. This will be communicated to us – either directly or through their behaviour – and will affect our self-image, which in turn influences our behaviour. The cycle evolves and changes over time.

Jane

In a role-play exercise on a public management course Jane was really surprised to be nominated by the other participants

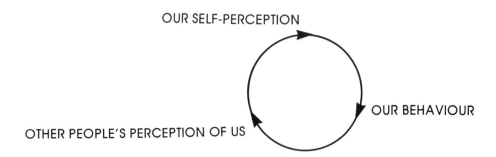

to play the Headteacher. Her senior colleagues had never indicated that she had worthy ideas and competencies. They had resisted her attempts to participate in whole school issues and decision-making. She had come to feel that she was unlikely to reach a headteacher's position. She had applied for a few promoted posts in and out of her school and had never been shortlisted so had assumed she was not up to it. Her self-perception, influenced by the perception and behaviour of others, led her to behave in a low-profile and unassertive way, which in itself generated the belief in others that she was not management material. Over time she had lost confidence in her abilities and her personal power had eroded.

Christa

Christa was running a time management course for senior managers. Over a number of courses she had built up a very good relationship with them as a consultant and trainer. On this occasion, however, the course was not going so well. 'I felt as if my credibility was gradually diminishing in their eyes and my answers to their questions became vague. It was the first time I was running the course, yet I knew my material thoroughly. I thought I've got to stop this. I acted with more direction and authority, I sharpened my body language and responded with greater energy. Their response to me completely changed as I *changed my approach, and the course actually concluded very positively for all of us.'*

OUR SELF-PERCEPTION

Personal power is directly linked to how we see ourself – our self-perception. How we see ourselves will be influenced by:

- our level of self-awareness
- beliefs about ourself and what we have learned about our abilities
- the rights and responsibilities we give ourself in relation to others
- how confident we feel in our capacity to learn
- our willingness to receive praise and acknowledge our successes
- the extent to which we feel we can influence our lives
- the extent to which we have a firm sense of self
- how our personal authority relates to the authority we perceive in others

Angharad

Angharad is the marketing director for a manufacturing company. 'I was asked to give a talk to a group of managers on a course one evening. At the end of the talk there was a five second silence followed by applause. I read this to mean they did not like my talk, I had not struck a chord with them and had wasted their time. As soon as the applause was over and I had taken a couple of questions I literally ran out of the room, got in my car and drove.

'A few days later I received a kind letter from the course leader stating how much they had enjoyed the talk. She also

125

supplied a sheet of comments from the delegates – they were fantastic. I could not believe how much they had appreciated it. I had interpreted their reaction as negative. My own lack of belief in myself was the factor that destroyed the evening for me.'

A common tendency amongst women is automatically to think of themselves in a less positive way than is the case. Low self-perception causes us to hear selectively, receiving only negative messages and rejecting positive praise or compliments. In addition, such an attitude leads us to assume that everyone else feels better about themselves than we do, so we communicate less openly as we fear it will expose us to a direct comparison. We can become more withdrawn and tentative, which fuels our undervaluing of ourselves. So the cycle continues.

The reasons for this are complex and could make a book themselves. Briefly, as our self-perception starts to develop in infancy and continues through our childhood – in the family and in school – and from our experiences at work, the seeds of low self-worth can be sown at any stage, stunting our growth to healthy self-esteem.

As children we send out a sense of ourselves, rather like the rays from a lighthouse. Just as a beam of light will disperse to the horizon if it is not reflected back from a solid object, so our sense of self diminishes if the beam of who we are is not met with acknowledgement, acceptance and validation. For example, adults frequently criticise children in a personal way saying: 'You are so stupid', rather than citing what was done that was wrong. At work it is common that we are told what we have not done well than what we have done well. As women, we are often taught to defer to men, to wait for them to take the first move and not to blow our own trumpets. Put-downs, low personal evaluation of us by others and negative messages about our competencies, plus an implied code that others are more important, fuel a downward cycle. Carrying around low self-worth as an adult can tap into our sense of childhood and lead us to feel we are acting like a child.

Self-esteem and self-confidence

High self-esteem is characterised by an innate feeling of worth, self-approval and value. It is the springboard that enables us to make choices that affect our life and career direction, the people we choose as partners and friends, the type of organisation we work for and the salary we think we deserve. It will determine what behaviour is acceptable and unacceptable to us and our ability to negotiate in the interests of ourself, our team and our organisation.

With low self-esteem, by contrast, we feel less good about ourself and limited in our choices about what we can say and do interpersonally and the options available to us in our life.(Self-esteem is different from the esteem that we get from external things, like a nice home, material possessions or status.These might make us feel good, but they do not in themselves create self-esteem.)

Many people confuse self-esteem with self-confidence and try to tackle the latter without attention to its basis. Whereas self-esteem is internal, confidence is an outer expression. The two can reflect the same or quite different feelings. Those who appear confident may or may not be so inside. For example, when giving a presentation, confidence can be a facade telling the world we are in control and competent when in fact we are terrified inside. In such circumstances, self-confidence relies heavily on the word 'con'.

To understand this further it is helpful to think of ourselves as a beautiful plant or flower, with what is seen above the ground representing the image we present to the world. For our self-confidence to grow we have to fertilise the roots of the plant – our self-esteem. The practical tips in this chapter are all methods of nourishing our self-esteem roots and can help us to develop that wonderful sense of liking and approving of ourself.

> *   *'By meeting more senior women and hearing their experience I realise I am capable of so much more – if they can achieve their career goals why shouldn't I.'*
> *   *'Carrying out an assessment of my strengths and weaknesses helped me to realise that I am not more or less important than anyone else but equally as valid and valuable.'*
> *   *'I attended an important business trip instead of my manager and was just myself – and it was very successful.'*

> *   *'Asking for a salary increase and really believing I am entitled to it increased my sense of self-worth.'*
> *   *'I know for me to be really effective I need at least three holiday breaks a year. I work really hard, so I make sure I get them.'*
> *   *'I recognised that getting people to help me was not a reflection of my inability but an empowering acknowledgement of my strengths and weaknesses. I have learnt to work to my strengths and recognise the strengths of others to redress the balance of my weaknesses.'*
> *   *'Everytime I feel fearful I think "This is just a feeling – who is in charge, me or my fear?" By facing the fear I become more empowered.'*

OUR BEHAVIOUR

The way we behave will determine how people treat us. Important points to consider are:

*   In a difficult situation, do we behave as if we are confident or lacking confidence?
*   Do we act and thus create the impression that we are competent or incompetent?
*   Do we speak up when taken advantage of or do we let people walk all over us?
*   Do we automatically put ourselves down, telling others of our incapabilities?
*   Do we choose to engage in activities that give us energy or sap our confidence?

- Do we find it difficult to accept compliments or positive feedback?
- Do we avoid expressing our views in meetings?
- Do we ask for what we want?

---

* *'I had to get out of the habit of apologising every time I asked a question. Just because I was asking it did not mean it was stupid.'*
* *'In meetings I used to die inside and consequently I would not look up when I spoke. I could not understand why people would not take me seriously. When I changed my tone of voice and looked the others in the eye I received a different reaction.'*
* *'Whenever someone gave me a compliment I would make such a big deal about how whatever they said wasn't true or that what I was wearing was not that good that people stopped giving them to me. I really believed that was what you had to do to show you are modest. I hadn't realised I was putting myself and the other person down.'*

Often our behaviour has become automatic; we do not analyse what we are doing, so carry on out of habit. Such habitual behaviour will have

arisen from our beliefs about what is appropriate or acceptable in situations – our interpersonal entitlement. We will have absorbed
this interpersonal framework during our lives as
a guide to new situations. Unfortunately our
behaviour can actually diminish our personal
power in the eyes of others.

Lucinda

*Lucinda is the chief executive of a large national charity. 'The
chairperson of my board of governors is a woman. She has a
habit of deferring to the men on virtually all the matters on the
agenda. When we started working together I found it really irritating and quite disconcerting, until a friend pointed it out to me
that maybe this has a lot to do with her conditioning. She
honestly believes that the men will know best because they are
the men.'*

Bumni

*A senior woman manager commented on the different ways
men and women negotiated the salary for a new job which she
felt reflected their self-beliefs. 'It is notable that the men generally look me in the eye and assertively ask for the middle to
top end salary range. The equally technically competent women
often get embarrassed and ask for the bottom to middle end of
the salary range. The view could be that they are less capable.
Incidentally, if this is generally the case for women, it must be
a factor in our national statistics which say we earn 70% of our
male equivalents.'*

Awareness of our own behaviour and its implications for others' perceptions of us is the first
step if we are to shift to communicating in ways
we would like. This theme is extended in
Chapter 5.

OTHERS' PERCEPTION

In addition to its relationship with behaviour, our personal power is also influenced by others' perception of us. If someone holds us in high esteem and encourages us to believe in ourselves we will tend to respond to that. Conversely, others' limited expectations of us can lead us to believe that we are less capable than we actually are.

> * *'Because my partner had told me that I was no good so many times I really began to believe it. It began to affect my work and my other relationships with people. I allowed a lot of people to walk all over me because I lost sight of my own worth. Now I am out of the relationship and I can see how destructive it was.'*
> * *'My mother is genuinely surprised that I have a successful career and recently told me, how she had never thought that I would have done so well.'*
> * *'My boss kept telling me I was hopeless at every opportunity. Only when I discussed it with a colleague did I realise how I had come to believe it and given him all the power in the relationship. I knew if I stayed in the department the situation would get worse. So I asked for an immediate transfer.'*

Other people's perception of us will vary in its accuracy and appropriateness and can be created by:

- our behaviour
- our track record
- hearsay
- others' own beliefs and views, values and prejudices

The extent to which we believe others' views and are influenced by them will depend on our perception of those people.

Sometimes we will interpret others' perceptions of us from their behaviour and we can be accurate or inaccurate in this. Testing the evidence is also a vital tool. We need to be mindful of those views we accept wholesale, those we select from and those we reject. The people upon whose views we are basing our own opinion will be a factor, and this is covered later.

Many of us have areas of significant self-doubt – the points about which we are very sensitive and so overact when they are commented on. If we allow other people to undermine us and believe it we are handing them our power on a plate. Similarly we disempower ourselves by mistakenly thinking that we need to conform to certain styles or behaviours in order to be attractive (or that being attractive to others generally is important!).

Allowing others too great an influence in our self-perception is a major problem. Clearly we need to take soundings, but for personal power we need to acknowledge the gap between others' views of what we should do or be and our own views; we cannot do this unless we have developed confidence in our own views. We should not assume that others have some authority to determine what we should do, and we can disempower ourselves with anxiety by worrying about how others see us. Conversely our inner robustness and personal sense of self-worth will grow as we take responsibility for our actions. This in itself will give us more confidence.

---

* *'I realised that all my life I had been wondering if what I was doing was OK, if other people would find it acceptable.'*
* *'I tried so hard to please people and wanted to be liked.'*
* *'I could never make a decision without checking it out with everyone. I know this can be important, but there comes a point when you have to trust your instinct and experience.'*
* *'Looking back it's almost as if everyone else had the monopoly on the good ideas and the right thing to do. If they said it convincingly enough I was naive enough to believe them and ultimately gave them all my power.'*
* *'I went to career counsellor who told me she was surprised I had done so well at my A levels. According to her psychometrics tests I was not academic. I went on to get an honours degree.'*

> *   'My first boss told me I would never get on as I had a problem with attention to detail. At the time I was so angry I thought I would show her. Six months later I was promoted because of the quality of my work.'

WHAT CAN WE DO TO DEVELOP PERSONAL POWER?

Rather than allowing others all the power in determining our personal power, we need to reclaim our influence in the matter. Realistically we cannot expect to change other people. However we can change the way we see ourselves and our behaviour and in turn influence the perception of others. The cycle of personal power allows our perception to change, which provides a strong base upon which we can continue to build.

Inevitably, developing our personal power – which only we can take responsibility for – entails pushing back boundaries. Deciding how we are going to do this involves reference to the three dimensions of self-perception, behaviour and others' perception and can be inspired by a sense of what helps us to feel powerful.

EXERCISE
PERSONAL POWER

• Complete the following statement with as many responses as you wish:

I feel powerful when . . .

DEFINE AND BELIEVE IN A CODE OF RIGHTS AND RESPONSIBILITIES

Our personal power is directly linked to our sense of entitlement. Our beliefs regarding those things we feel we are entitled to do or have in our lives make up our personal code of rights. These rights carry with them responsibilities too. These rights and responsibilities will have been acquired from:

- our family upbringing
- our social conditioning
- our schooling and workplace experience
- the patterns in our relationships
- gender and cultural influences

Gloria

Gloria was brought up in a home where children were seen and not heard. This message was reinforced at school where some teachers would publicly humiliate those who gave the wrong answer. 'If we gave the right answer we would receive no acknowledgement or praise, it was just expected. I think this has influenced my beliefs in what I am entitled to do and I find it really difficult to speak up for myself in public.'

Val

Val works as a teacher. 'For a long time I did not believe I was entitled to a life outside of school during term time. I would think nothing of working until 11.30 pm every night. The head teacher at my first school was a workaholic and set the trend for everyone else. As I did not know any other way I really thought this is what is expected of me – and that I was the problem because I could not cope.'

Because we can sometimes be uncertain about what we believe our rights and responsibilities are in any situation, defining and working on them can help. A group of women on the Pepperell Management Development Course developed the following list of rights. These represent areas where difficulties were experienced, either in confidence in the right or in its acceptance by others. Although we have grouped them they are not in any particular order.

The right to be happy and enjoy life
The right to my own time and space
The right to have a family and a career
The right to be treated as my own person
The right to be myself

The right to equality of opportunity
The right to walk without fear
The right to privacy
The right not to be stereotyped

The right to my own views, feelings, values, opinions and beliefs
The right to be listened to
The right not to accept what others say
The right to say 'yes' or 'no'
The right to negotiate
The right to disagree
The right to compromise

The right to express my feelings
The right to question
The right to complain
The right to change my mind
The right to ask for help

137

*The right not to live up to my own or others
expectations*
The right to make mistakes
*The right to choose when I work outside con-
tracted hours*
The right to spare time
The right to party!

It is one thing to recognise on an intellectual
level that we have any specific rights; it can be
difficult to accept them on an emotional level
when we are dealing with a difficult situation.
Having clarified our own code of rights in our
mind, we need to work towards:

• believing them emotionally
• acting as if we believe them

Believing them does not mean we can change
other people or that we can expect them to
accept our rights. However, it can give us
greater confidence when others treat us in ways
we find unacceptable by enabling us to realise
that what is going on reflects their perspective
and not our own.

EXERCISE –
YOUR OWN RIGHTS

• Draft your own personal code of rights.
• Work towards accepting them in your
  feelings and actions.
• If you find this difficult, putting the sentence 'I do not have the right to . . .' in
  front of a right can change the picture.

If we do not want to be aggressive about our rights, we need to acknowledge two points:
- if we have these rights, other people have them too
- with our rights we have responsibilities

Examples of responsibilities:

| RIGHT | To be listened to |
| RESPONSIBILITY | To talk clearly and listen to others |

RIGHT	To make mistakes
RESPONSIBILITY	To learn from mistakes
	To accept the consequences of my mistakes

| RIGHT | To express my feelings |
| RESPONSIBILITY | To be responsible for the consequences |

RIGHT	To my own time and space
RESPONSIBILITY	To be clear cut with you about my need
	To respect your right to time and space

Clarity about our rights and responsibilities helps us:
- not to give away our personal power
- not to do what everyone else expects us to do, without regard or thought to what we need or believe
- not to become what we think people will want us to be.

STOP THINKING NEGATIVELY

It is often easier to dwell on what we cannot do rather than focus on what we can. Negative-thinking can diminish our sense of self-worth and stop us recognising all those things we have achieved and are capable of achieving. It can be a habit of which we are not consciously aware.

Mary

Mary is a marketing executive for a finance company. 'I used to have sleepless nights before my first few meetings with the advertising agency because I was so worried about them know-ing more than me, in case I wasted the company's money or made a mistake. Then one day the penny dropped – of course they know more than me – that's why we employ them for their expertise. The meetings are far more productive because I am less defensive and suspicious.'

Blaming ourselves for anything and everything negative that happens is another way we talk ouselves down. Similarly, by comparing our-selves negatively with others, we undermine ourselves and progressively destroy our power.

Louise

Louise had a habit of putting herself down. It was so deeply ingrained that she didn't even realise how often she was making self-derogoratory comments. A good friend at work pointed this pattern out and bought her a book to write in one achievement every day. 'At first it was really difficult to identify anything but through persistence and a real desire to change my perception of myself it has become easier. Just the effort of trying to think of something positive about myself has raised my awareness of how negative I can be and has forced me to stop putting myself down.'

> ### EXERCISE –
> ### STOP THE AUTOMATIC NEGATIVE
>
> - If you catch yourself thinking negatively about yourself in a situation, stop – and allow the negative thought to go.
> - Some people visualise themselves putting it to one side or in a box.
> - Work towards replacing negative thoughts with more positive ones.

Using our inner voice

The inward dialogue of our inner voice will often be more apparent before an unknown or undesirable event. We can persuade ourselves in advance that the situation will be dreadful and if we do this well enough we can almost guarantee a real disaster! In anticipation of a difficult meeting our inner conversation could go like this:

* I know this presentation will be hopeless. They're all senior managers and experts and will expect an in-depth and really slick presentation. I hate presentations. I know the last one I did was okay, but it wasn't brilliant. Why did I ever agree to do this? I'm going to make such a fool of myself. They'll ask me questions that I've never dreamt of. It will ruin my credibility and reputation.

Of course this negative thinking easily fulfils

141

itself by impacting on our performance at the meeting.

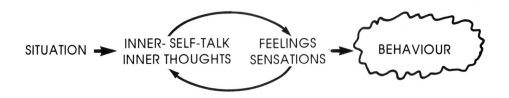

However, we can coach ourselves to change the inner messages and look more positively at a given situation. Our thoughts could go like this:

* I feel really nervous about this presentation, which is understandable. I always do but I'll manage. They've asked me because I know a lot about this particular issue. Even if there are other experts there it doesn't matter because we all have different experiences of the subject. I know from previous experience I perform a lot better if I rehearse. I'm really going to give it my best shot. I can gain a lot of kudos from doing this, but absolutely nothing if I don't even try.

Working with the inner voice requires a conscious choice to talk ourselves up – to focus on the positive. This is not about being over-positive or optimistic, but being aware of our thinking and having a more balanced view.

SITUATION → POSITIVE INNER THOUGHTS AND SELF-TALK ⟷ FEEL COMFORTABLE AND RELAXED → ASSERTIVE BEHAVIOUR

EXERCISE –
COACH YOURSELF UP

- Before a difficult situation, stop to notice the negative inner dialogue you are creating.
- Change it so that your thoughts support you instead of undermining you.

Positive affirmations

In addition to the inner dialogue before an event, many of us regularly talk ourselves down with negative, undermining statements about our worth or value.

They may be the messages we received as a little girl from teachers, parents and other relatives. For example:

* *I'm so stupid.*
* *Trust me to make a mistake.*
* *I'm so fat and ugly.*
* *I'm useless, so what's the point.*

We can carry these messages with us into adulthood and never question them because when we

143

were small we thought adults knew best. When we are in a difficult or fearful situation at work and we feel as if we are not coping, the messages get louder!

We have a choice about the messages we give ourselves. We can replace these negative messages with something positive – even if we don't actually believe it. The belief will come in time. These positive messages need to be said in the present tense and state what we are, not what we are not. For example:

* I am intelligent.
* I am competent and effective.
* I am attractive and confident.
* I am capable and powerful.

How we think of ourselves will in turn have an impact on our feelings about ourselves and our behaviour, and ultimately on the way others see us.

Donna

'Through reading various books on developing the power of positive thinking I thought it was about time I started to apply the principles. The organisation was going through a restructure and people generally were feeling very insecure and negative. It could have been so easy for me to have got sucked into it. I made a point every day as I walked from the bus stop to the office to say repeatedly in myself "I am a bright, confident, postive, successful woman and only good things can happen to me."

'As soon as I saw anyone I would smile deliberately at them. The effect on them and on me was remarkable. By starting out positively it coloured the rest of the day. The restructure was nowhere near as bad as it could have been and my boss actually commented on how my attitude had helped him and a lot of other people. The important thing for me is to keep it up.'

Another tool to switch from negative to positive is to be aware of what we are saying to ourself, stop saying it and say something else.

---

* 'When I catch myself beating myself over the head when something goes wrong I have learnt to sit back and look at what has gone well instead.'
* 'In a difficult situation when I am talking myself down I say to myself that I'm not a helpless child, I'm a powerful and successful adult now.'
* 'After a dreadful day when everything had gone badly – from oversleeping, to leaving my handbag in a cab, to having to cancel an important meeting – I felt that nothing had been positive at all. Then I decided that I hadn't actually let it get me down – I had just got on with the day.'

Looking for the positive

It is positive at the end of a day to take stock of all the things we have done well or that have gone smoothly. Even if we think that they should have gone smoothly because that is what is expected, we can still acknowledge our part in them and in so doing reinforce our sense of self-worth. Turning a negative around so that we look at in a more positive frame is also important in this process. It can prove helpful to

145

choose an especially pleasing book in which to review and celebrate our achievements.

EXERCISE –
REVIEWING OUR ACHIEVEMENTS

- Every day make time to reflect on: - what you actually achieved- what you are proud of
- If you find yourself focusing on the less positive things, acknowledge any error, failure or mistake and what you can learn from it.
- Let go of what you have not managed to do and schedule it in for the next day. Remember we can only achieve 12 hours' activity in 12 hours.

Our response to failure

The way we handle failure can either help us grow or demolish us.

- Do we give ourselves permission to fail – seeing it as not the end of the world, but as a setback that needs to be overcome or learnt from, so we can be more effective?
- Do we treat failure as a terrible indictment of our worth as a human being and punish ourselves for being so inadequate?

Ways of responding to failure that diminish us will have been learnt through experience and it is possible to relearn them. Recognising that making a mistake is exactly that – a mistake – is a more positive attitude to adopt. Failure can teach us positive things about ourself, including the strength revealed in the struggle we have had.

> *   'It was watching my little girl learn how to walk that I was struck by the fact that she had no sense of failure every time she fell down. I could see clearly that my attitude to failure has been a learnt response and not something that I was born with – in this case I could change it into something positive.'

If we are frightened of failure because of how it affects our sense of self-worth we will never try new things or push back our boundaries. This attitude will adversely affect our self-worth. We have to be prepared to take risks if we want to grow and that demands an approach that helps us support ourselves through failure and learn from our mistakes.

> *   'I failed my driving test six times. It got to the point when it was really embarrassing. I was determined to pass. I knew if I stopped trying I would never pass it. It was sheer determination that carried me through.'
> *   'I failed my professional exams. At first I thought I am such a failure. However, when I sat down and thought about it I had not worked for them as hard as I was capable of doing. I had to get it in perspective and see the truth of the matter – if I didn't work why should I pass?'

> ## EXERCISE –
> ## CONFRONTING FEAR OF FAILURE
>
> - List all the things that you would do if the outcome was guaranteed success.
> - List all the obstacles to success that you perceive.
> - Now look at the obstacles. Which of the obstacles could you have an influence on?

Handling success

What success means in our lives and how we handle it is the flip side of our reaction to failure.

Our personal meaning of success moves continuously. Our values change as we get older and what we wanted in the past will not necessarily be what we want now. Taking stock and seeing the shift helps us achieve success. Whether we perceive ourself as a winner or a loser will be influenced by our sense of personal power.

Underestimating our own worth and negatively evaluating our own work are commontendencies. Unfortunately they can be encouraged by others who point out only our downside. If we never receive praise we need to make a point of seeking it and giving it to ourselves.

> ## EXERCISE –
> ## POSITIVES NOT NEGATIVES
>
> - Keep a file of nice letters or positive comments about your work.
>
> - Copy praise to your boss.
>
> - Pin a good comment on your notice board.
>
> - Talk about the achievements of people in your team.
>
> - Use these to boost yourself at times you feel low.

The imposter phenomenon is the fear that someone will find us out and realise that we are a fraud. The term was coined by Clance and Imes who found the phenomenon to be particularly prevalent among a select sample of high-achieving women who, despite their achievements, did not feel inside that they were successful (Clance & O'Toole 1988). We have heard many other women reporting this feeling and the associated fear of discovery. The tendency is to attribute all success to luck, not acknowledge hard work and to deny our ability. Clearly it is a way we disempower ourselves.

149

* *'I'm only in this position because I was lucky enough to be in the right place at the right time.'*
* *'Once they find out I've only been working in this area for two years they will not want to know.'*
* *'I'm on this board because I'm the token woman, not because I've got anything to contribute.'*
* *'Just because I've written a paper on this area it doesn't make me the expert.'*
* *'How could they appoint me? I know as soon as I've been in the job for a while they'll think they've made a big mistake.'*
* *'All of these people are older than me – they probably know far more about this than I do.'*

Sometimes we feel that we are not entitled to success, that it will not come to someone like us. Embracing our ambivalence – wanting success but not allowing it – can be helped by positive role models who demonstrate what is possible. On the other hand, constant striving for success and the external evaluation it supplies can be a way of compensating for a low sense of self-worth. We need to believe that we deserve success on our own terms.

Personal power flourishes when our actions cor-
respond with our values and intentions, yet acting with integrity carries the potential for risk.
At times we will be unpopular, we will have to
say 'no' to a certain things, we will not have
everyone's approval. It could mean in certain
circumstances that we actually lose business.

Antonia

*Antonia was responsible for invoicing a government depart-
ment for work that her organisation carried out. There was not
as much work as had been projected so the income for the contract would not be fulfilled. 'The chief executive concerned
decided that I would have to falsify some invoices to raise
revenue levels. I was told to create some invoices for work we
had not done. I was appalled at what she was asking me to do.
I refused to do it. For two weeks I was harangued by her. In the
end someone else prepared them and sent them off. They left
me alone after the incident, but my relationship was never the
same. In the end I left the organisation.'*

In return, acting with integrity will ensure
peace of mind, a growth in our self-esteem, the
respect of the majority of people and the perception by others that we are professional and
honest in all of our affairs. We will not waste
energy covering our tracks or having sleepless
nights.

> * *'I realised the gossip in the team was destroying everyone's trust. I couldn't change the rest of them but I could make a decision to stop joining in.'*
> * *'Backing my colleague who was being sexually harassed by the boss was the most difficult decision I've had to take and yet I knew I could not live with myself if I did not support her.'*
> * *'My sleepless nights were caused by my unfulfilled promises to colleagues and clients. It was exhausting trying to justify what I had not done because I had taken on too much. Speaking up about my time limitations really made a difference.'*
> * *'Refusing to get involved with a client because they wanted to close down their union was a great risk and yet for me I would not have done a good job and would have hated coming to work.'*

TRUST OUR CAPACITY TO LEARN

One way to look at something we cannot do is to see it as our next challenge, rather than as a failure on our part as a human being.

Ros

Ros, a recruitment consultant, believes many women only feel confident in job applications if they believe that they can do at least 80% of the role's demands. By contrast men will usually apply if they believe that they can do about 60% of it.

'The men I see seem to have this belief that their capacity to learn will carry them through and enable them to pick up the bits they don't know. The women seem to want an absolute guarantee that they can handle it all. This stops them applying for jobs they would be perfectly capable of doing and makes them diffident at interview. I think this is one reason why we still have very few women managers.'

Trusting our capacity to learn and taking steps to demonstrate it will grow our personal power.

Tessa

Tessa works in a large retail group. 'I started out as a computer programmer. I decided to adopt a policy of always applying for jobs I couldn't do in order to build up my skills base and learn about the organisation in the process. I knew the senior managers would not consider me unless they had come into contact with me before the the interviews. I became a staff counsellor, joined the job evaluation panel as the staff representative and joined the organisation's policy group. These activities provided me with a range of skills I would not be able to acquire through my normal job. They have raised my profile with senior managers so they know what I am capable of learning and achieving. They gave me useful insight into how to approach the organisation for funding for my MBA programme. I think it's pointless to say "what if I fail?" How will I know if I don't have a go. As a result of this attitude I have been promoted several times because I am perceived to be an all-rounder and someone who is committed to the organisation and enjoys her work.'

FACE THE SPIDERS IN THE BATH

Anxiety and fear are normal feelings and yet they can eat away at our personal power by keeping us in safe zones, avoiding the action we desire. They can also encourage us to procrastinate. The things we are putting off are rarely as bad as we think they will be, even if they are, we will survive. Sir Peter White, in his book *Preparing for the Top*, talks about dealing with the most difficult thing we have on our minds first thing in the morning so that we can get on with the rest of the day. Whatever is dominating our thoughts will not go away until we tackle it.

The only way to overcome fear is to experience it and work through it. It will pass eventually, although at the time we are going through a difficult period or situation it does not feel like it! Often the fear itself is greater than the thing we are frightened of.

Brian Keenan, who was held hostage in Beirut for five years, speaks of fear as a 'meaningless object which contaminates us, bred in ourselves by ourselves. Courage is controlling our fearfulness. Courageous understanding comes once you learn and know that fear diminishes as you yourself extinguish it.'

Irene
Irene has a daughter with severe learning difficulties and autism. 'I knew from networking with other parents, reading about the different types of problems experienced by children like my daughter, and my intuition, that she was autistic. The problem for me was the attitude of the consultant paediatrician. He was adamant that she was not autistic.

'It went against everything I had been taught not to question the experts or authority, but deep down inside I knew I was right. I knew he was a good man, but I had to trust my instincts. Every time we met, although I was really afraid, I kept insisting that I wanted a second opinion. He implied I was neurotic and

154

over-protective. It was only when I got the support of my daughter's school that he finally agreed to refer her to another hospital. It turned out I was correct. This was not only a really important turning point for my daughter, as she now has the right education and care, but it was also very important for me. I have learnt to trust my instincts and not let my fear of authority get in the way of what I believe to be right.'

Personal power develops as we learn that we can tackle the things that we are fearful of. The expression 'say yes and panic later' can inspire us to accept the challenges that will stretch us and that will, in the process, increase our confidence and self-esteem. By pushing back boundaries in a controlled way – ensuring that we have adequate preparation time for the task and seeking the support and help that will assist us to success – we shift our self-perception, and others' perception of us.

Lisa

Lisa is a consultant in the National Health Service. 'The restructure in the NHS has given me the opportunity to become a manager of a department and I am going to receive further management and financial management training. However, I am terrified of the financial side. I have always let my husband look after our finances but the only way I am going to overcome this fear is by having a go at understanding and managing our own finances. He is very resistant to handing over control, but gradually he is coming round. By the time I have to manage the department budget I will be more comfortable with the idea.'

SET LIMITS

Certain tasks may seem to be opportunities but actually have no potential to extend our personal power. Some tasks in fact deplete personal

155

power because they keep us working in restricted areas or exhaust us. Through overload. While we aim to develop ourselves through pushing out boundaries we need to ensure that we do not just accept tasks that benefit only others or but in fact select activities that are in themselves also beneficial to us.

The process of deciding whether to take on a task or not can be assisted by defining no-go areas that determine our limits and help define the boundaries between us and others. They are the culmination of forethought and insight into what we need to be effective. Obviously they will not be completely rigid, causing us to turn down a wonderful or enjoyable opportunity. In these circumstances we would have to consider the trade-offs. What no-go areas do is provide a frame of reference that makes us assess what is asked of us and not respond automatically without thought for the implications or consequences.

With clarity about our boundaries we can work to maintain them. One problem might be taking too much responsibility for others. Signs of this would be over-responsiveness to the concerns of other people.

Obviously this will be legitimate in some relationships but women can often overdo it – picking up others' concerns and blaming themselves and trying to make it better. Clarifying the extent of our responsibility for and to others and of theirs to us can contribute to our personal power.

> * 'Always keeping two evenings a week free for the family'
> * 'Not taking work home except in an emergency'
> * 'Not lending my car to anyone without a really good reason'
> * 'Questioning extra work that is asked of me'
> * 'Not accepting travelling demands for work which may require me to drive when really tired'

EXERCISE – NO-GO AREAS

* Decide your own no-go areas and test them out.
  They can be adjusted during the testing but then should be quite firm.
* See how they help you assess requests.

TAKE CARE OF OURSELVES

Women frequently say 'yes' to tasks that adversely affect their quality of life and do not satisfy their personal career aspirations. Personal power and good self-esteem are built up when we treat ourselves well and believe we deserve to be treated well.

Keeping a focus on ourselves involves looking at every aspect of our life and making sure we have time for ourself so that we can also have-time for others. The only person who can ensure this is us.

In addition to following the tips explored in Chapter 3, we must learn to recognise the warning signs that we are doing too much and not recharging ourselves. By seeing them as useful and acting on them positively we can head off exhaustion and burn-out, when we are effective for no one.

---

*   *'If I start to have more than three or four sleepless nights or wake up too early consecutively over a period of a few days I know something is wrong.'*
*   *'I get eczema on my hands when things are starting to get out of control.'*
*   *'My acne comes back if I am under a lot of pressure and know I need to stop.'*
*   *'I stutter when I'm not coping.'*
*   *'I start writing endless lists when things are getting too hectic.'*
*   *'When my moods seem more extreme and changeable I know that I have to do something.'*
*   *'I take frequent headaches as a warning sign.'*

EXERCISE – RECOGNISE THE WARNING SIGNS

• Write down the physical, mental and emotional warning signals that you experienced the last time you were under great stress

GET THE PROBLEM OUT

Internal personal power is often eroded when we bottle problems up. Not all of us are able to let go of work and personal problems, which tend to get amplified at night and can steal the valuable rest we need for the next day. Lack of rest can lead to our being snappy and irritable, which will affect our relationships with colleagues, friends and family. One method that can help is to write down everything about the problem - especially how we feel. Twenty minutes of frantic scribbling often transfers the problem onto paper, where it can stay until the next day. A more balanced perspective on how to address our thorny issue may well emerge when we wake up.

BUILD UP A SUPPORT NETWORK

The 'macho' attitude to a problem or difficult time is that we should be able to handle it by ourselves. This is unrealistic and self-indulgent and stops us finding solutions.

Phyllis

Phyllis works as a personnel manager in a large oil company. Her specialism is staff welfare and counselling. 'My work is very focused on looking after people and their needs. At times I am under great stress, especially as we are restructuring and making people redundant. Recently it has been really bad and this was exacerbated by my attitude. I have felt for a long time, because I'm in personnel I should be able to handle everything. By denying how vulnerable I can be I actually made the situation worse for myself.'

159

One of the most effective ways of dealing with a problem is to share it with someone. By talking it through we can often find a way around it or see alternative solutions. Accepting that we do not have to have all the answers is a real freedom in itself; it can be empowering to ask for help and receive support from others. By building up a support network we can learn to rebalance the giving and receiving. We can also get things done, get access to information and tap into professional expertise.

We need to choose people who we know will not betray our confidence or adversely affect our options or career prospects. We will also have to accept that it is reasonable and in fact positive for others to ask for and receive support from us.

EXERCISE –
SUPPORTIVE PEOPLE

- Write down the people at work and in your personal life who are good listeners and provide excellent support.

- You might think of the different types of support they give you and you give them, for example by:
  - challenging
  - being amusing
  - being trustworthy
  - unconditionally accepting
  - being reliable
  - being honest

> ## EXERCISE –
> ## NEGATIVE PEOPLE
>
> - Write down the names of people who affect your mood negatively
> - Identify the behaviour in them that you respond to. Plan how you can
>   - reduce contact with them
>   - react differently to them

MINIMISE CONTACT WITH NEGATIVE PEOPLE

Surrounding ourselves with positive, supportive people who believe in us and care about us is one aspect of taking care of ourselves. Colleagues or friends who are constantly moaning and whining and generating negative energy will eventually have an impact on our mood and our choices.

We cannot altogether avoid negative people, but we can minimise the contact we have with them.

THINK OF OURSELVES AS WE WOULD OF OTHERS

Frequently we expect more from ourselves than we do of others. We tolerate difficult situations that we would not expect others to accept. Helping colleagues and making their lives easier is great if we also do it for ourself.

161

> ### EXERCISE –
> ### TO MAKE MY JOB EASIER
>
> - Write down all the things you would want to do if you were preparing to hand over your job to someone else.
> - Now plan how you can do these things for yourself, to make your life easier and yourself more effective.

To identify ways of boosting our personal power we can think of ourself as we would a best friend.

Greta

'I spend quite a lot of money when I buy my friends presents. I will think nothing of traipsing round the shops for the perfect quality gift for them. It dawned on me on my last shopping trip for a friend that I never bother doing this for myself. I have decided that I deserve the best as well and from now on I'm going to be more choosey on how I spend my money on myself.'

> ## EXERCISE –
> ## IF I WAS MY BEST FRIEND I WOULD . . .
>
> - If I was my best friend I would . . .
> - Finish this sentence with a list and see if you can actually do these things for yourself.

> ## SUMMARY –
> ## PRACTICAL TIPS
>
> * Think about how you act
> * Check out others' perception of you
> * Be aware of your over-sensitive areas
> * Draw up a code of rights and responsibilities
> * Work on your positive inner voice
> * Develop your own positive affirmations
> * Review achievements
> * Collect positive comments
> * Trust your capacity to learn
> * Deal with the most difficult problems at the beginning of the day
> * Learn from mistakes
> * Build a support network
> * Be your own best friend

5

COMMUNICATING PERSONAL POWER

*Why then do women need power? Because
power is freedom. Power allows us to
accomplish what is important to us, in the
manner that we best see fit. It separates the
doers from the dreamers.*

(Patti F. Mancini)

PERSONAL POWER AND BEHAVIOUR

In Chapter 4 we have explored how to develop
inner personal power by working from the inside
on our beliefs and attitudes. In this chapter we
look at what is revealed through our behaviour,
and how, by behaving in certain ways, we can
continue to increase our personal power by
communicating it externally.

This does not mean that we will get everything
we want. It is not about manipulating others
and, whilst appearing to consider them, in fact
walking all over them. Personal power is created
by behaving in personally effective ways that we
feel good about and do not regret. Personal
effectiveness relies on interpersonal relationships that are based on a sense of equality, self-
worth and mutual respect.

THE IMPORTANCE OF RESPECT

'Respect' is crucial to personal effectiveness, yet
the word can have different connotations. Our

definition of respect is not based on what people do. Respect is not something that is earned – a common association – and does not imply approval. Nor does respecting someone mean that we admire or emulate them. Basic human respect in the context of personal effectiveness means deciding how we should treat people – and this will be different for each one of us – and behaving towards them in that way even when they behave towards us in ways we dislike or find difficult. It arises from our personal sense of rights (see Chapter 4).

Often we will respond according to the behaviour we receive – yet we give away our power if we allow others to determine how we should react to them. Respect allows us to make the norms that guide our behaviour, to dictate for ourselves our own unifying style. We then feel more personally powerful because:

* we and not they have chosen the behaviour
* we have behaved in ways of which we approve
* we are behaving with dignity

Sharon

Sharon works in the equal opportunities team within the personnel department of a large retail company. 'There is one woman who I find irritating. She has a habit of patronising me and implying that I'm not really that knowledgeable in the subject. She makes a point of going on about her qualifications and the fact she has worked for a larger organisation. Every time she speaks I feel like telling her to "get lost"; instead I'm really sarcastic.

165

'We had a new member of the team join us and she pointed out to me that my reaction aggravated the situation. She also got me to think about my colleague's perspective and feelings of confidence. I've stopped reacting and just deal with the topic we are discussing rather than making sarcastic comments. The relationship isn't perfect, but it has improved and I feel better about the way I'm handling it.'

INTERPERSONAL POWER

We train people how to treat us. The power we communicate externally will affect how others see us, which in turn influences the way we see ourself and our ability to behave in personally effective ways.

> * 'They never ask me my opinion; just because I'm quiet it doesn't mean I don't have an opinion.'
> * 'I know I'm new to the department but they should make the effort to get to know me. How can they say I'm aloof?'
> * 'I hate networking – no one ever speaks to me.'
> * 'Just because I've lost my temper a couple of times, they don't tell me what's going on!'

We cannot change another person or their behaviour, but we can change our own behaviour and the way we respond to others, thus influencing their perception of us and reaction to us. This is a way into powerful relationships that help us to feel good and claim our personal power.

* 'When I spoke up at that meeting they actually listened to what I had to say.'
* 'Saying "no" to working late again has made all the difference – my manager has started to organise her work more efficiently.'
* 'Telling my colleague how difficult it is for me to complete my work when he got the information to me late has really helped. He hadn't realised the problems it caused me.'
* 'The regular one-to-one meetings I asked for have made my working life so much easier.'
* 'I can see that dealing with that customer's anger at the time has improved our relationship with him. We could have lost him for good if I had done my usual thing and over-reacted.'
* 'By addressing the problems as they come up our teamworking has really improved.'

OUR CHOICE IN BEHAVIOUR

We may well feel that our behaviour is out of our power, but we do have a choice in the way we behave.

Awareness of our own and others' behaviour is the starting point for breaking behavioural habits. This does not mean that we are judging the behaviour, rather that through the practice of observation we learn to identify it. We may feel that another person's behaviour is in a way caused by us. The regular process of recognition helps us to see that the behaviour is theirs and not ours. We can take responsibility only for our own actions.

Eventually, with heightened sensitivity, understanding and skill, we can choose how we will behave. The momentary pause, to recognise and identify the behaviour we are dealing with, enables us to suppress our usual reaction and respond appropriately by choice. We can decide to behave differently, and this may include stopping our reactions to the behaviour displayed by others. We will not change overnight; in fact the process needs to be gradual if we are not to alarm the people around us!

DIFFERENT BEHAVIOUR TYPES

Understanding the ways we behave is helped by looking at the different types of behaviour that people can exercise. There are four broad types or categories of behaviour:

- directly aggressive behaviour
- indirectly aggressive behaviour (sometimes known as manipulative)
- passive behaviour (sometimes known as non-assertive)
- assertive behaviour (also referred to as personal effectiveness)

It is important to appreciate that these are not personality types but behavioural styles that we will have learnt. No one person behaves in one way. Whilst we might display one behaviour predominantly, particularly when under stress,

we will generally dip in and out of all four in
different situations, depending on the circumstances. The following are characteristics of the
behaviour types. They may seem a bit like car-
icatures, but this is for ease of recognition.

BEHAVIOUR TYPE	BEHAVIOUR DESCRIPTION	COMMON REACTIONS
Aggressive	Arrogant	Fearful
	Threatening	Defensive
	Blaming	Aggressive
	Loud	Hurt
	Intimidating	Humiliated
	Violent	Resentful
	Superior	

* *You made a fool of me in front of those people and I won't
  have it, I won't have it – do you hear me you idiot!*

* *I didn't make a fool of you, you're more than capable of
  doing that by yourself. How dare you speak to me like
  that!*

Manipulative or Indirectly Aggressive	Sarcastic	Confused
	Silent	Frustrated
	treatment	Guilty
	Obsequious	Angry
	Cunning	Distrustful
	Devious	Flattered
	Sulking	

* *So do you think it was an intelligent course of action to promise them delivery tomorrow when you know we have to get this job out? Tell me what are you planning on doing – working through the night!*

* *If no one else will do it I suppose it will just have to be me.*

Passive	Uses guilt	Frustrated
	Avoidance	Resentful
	Victim	Aggressive
	syndrome	Exasperated
	Deferring	Inhibited

* *I'm so sorry I didn't get the report done on time. I really am sorry but I have had a lot of problems with my staff. They're causing me a lot of worry at the moment. I'm usually quite efficient. It's just recently because of the restructure they've been playing me up – coming in late, taking long lunch hours . . . I don't know what to do.*

* *I really don't mind. You tell me what I should do in this circumstance.*

Assertive or Personally Effective	Self-contained	Trustful
	Acts with	Respectful
	Integrity	Confident
	Responsible	Comfortable
	Self-confident	Envious
	Sincere	Incompetent
	Direct	

* *I am having problems writing this report. Could I have ten minutes of your time to clarify the objectives?*

* *At the moment it's not convenient; however, if you would like to come and see me in an hour's time, we could talk then.*

<u>EXERCISE -</u>
<u>RECOGNISING OUR BEHAVIOUR AND OUR</u>
<u>REACTIONS TO OTHERS' BEHAVIOUR</u>

- Using the lists above, over a period of time be alert to behaviour.

- Identify the typical behaviours of people you come into contact with.

- Identify in what situations and with whom you display the behaviour types

- Identify the specific behaviours that you find more difficult to deal with and your reactions to them.

BEHAVIOURS AND RIGHTS

In Chapter 4 we identified the impact of a personal sense of rights and responsibilities on our self-perception; there is a distinct correlation between those rights we hold for ourselves and others and the behaviours we deploy. Generally we do not explicitly make this link and to change behaviour we need to be clear about the attitudinal underpinnings of what we do. Personal power is built on integrity – acting in ways that reflect our beliefs.

- When behaving aggressively we ignore the rights of others yet insist on our own
- When behaving passively we defer to the rights of others yet neglect our own

- When behaving assertively we acknowledge and respect the rights of others as well as our own

BEHAVIOURS AND POWER

Each of the categories of behaviour has a different relationship with power (we are referring to interpersonal power and what is going on in the interaction and not to hierarchical power, which is based on positions in the organisation).

Power dynamics operate in most interactions. If we behave aggressively we are determined to get what we want and win – at any cost to the relationship. We attempt to be more powerful than the other person and will use ploys such as put-downs to exert that power so they feel less powerful. In aggressive mode we might say to a member of staff, 'You were useless the way you handled that client. No wonder we lost the account!'

A common misconception is that the aggressive style is powerful. In fact, because it seeks to overpower others, it generally stems from an internal sense of powerlessness. To feel powerful in this style it is necessary to dominate and reduce another's power because the power felt is only relative to others having less.

When behaving passively we perceive that the other person has more power and is intrinsically more important or more likely to get what they want, so we automatically defer to them. Behaving passively we might well put ourself down by saying 'I'm so stupid. I'm sure that it's all because of me that we lost that account.'

When we behave assertively we believe that

we are equally as powerful interpersonally and aim to address the real issues and reach some solution that partially satisfies all of us. An assertive statement would be, 'I am concerned that we lost that account and would like to look at the specific reasons why.'

BEHAVIOUR TYPES		
Aggressive (Direct and Indirect)	= Power over	= I win You lose
Passive	= Powerless	= I win You win
Assertive	= Power within Shared power	= I win You win

By definition, **assertive behaviour is behaviour that expresses the person's feelings, attitudes, wishes, opinions or rights with directness and honesty. It encompasses respect for the feelings, attitudes, wishes, opinions or rights of the other person.**

When we are assertive we tend to be happier with the way we have handled a situation. By not focusing on the power dynamic in the interaction we retain our personal power and respect that of the other person. Wonderfully, the more we work to achieve this the greater our sense of self worth – or power within.

Behaving assertively ensures that instead of reacting to the person's behaviour we are responding to the issue. While assertive behaviour is a useful general framework for day-to-day

173

interactions, it is also particularly valuable in difficult situations, for example:

- dealing with disagreements
- speaking up at meetings
- challenging unjustified criticism
- returning faulty goods
- negotiating a salary increase
- handling criticism
- saying 'no'
- confronting unreasonable behaviour
- tackling evasive behaviour
- stopping bullying and sexual harassment
- disciplining a member of staff

BEHAVING DIFFERENTLY

If we are to change a situation or influence someone's reaction to us we will need to behave differently in the situation. As Waldo Emerson said: 'If you keep doing what you're doing, you keep getting what you're getting'.' To understand how to change by becoming more assertive we need to highlight the situations that we feel we handle less than satisfactorily and in which behaving differently would lead to greater effectiveness.

Diana

Diana works as an accountant in a manufacturing company. She had recently been promoted from within the team to the position of a junior manager. The previous post holder was quite a bit older and had left a big impression on the other members of the team.

'I felt as if I was resented because I was young and relatively new to the company although I had better qualifications and I

174

had had some management experience. Because I felt so nervous about my position I tended to withdraw and communicate by memo. Any information I needed would always arrive late. There was no reason for this – I knew it and they knew it. Half the time I would end up doing it myself and resenting them.

'I finally decided I had had enough. I tackled each one individually, asking if there was a problem and each of them said there wasn't, so I said what I wanted. Just by asking outright for what I needed solved the problem. I had worn myself out worrying about the outcome when in actual fact their response to my reasonable requests needed to be dealt with. Since that time I've just been myself and whenever I have a problem I deal with it at the time.'

EXERCISE – IDENTIFYING SITUATIONS

• Identify three or four scenarios in which you would like to be more assertive, using the following guidelines to help:

With whom would you like to be assertive?
Consider the situations and the behaviour that you find difficult.
How would you describe your behaviour in these situations now – is it aggressive, manipulative or passive?
What do you think stops you being assertive?
What specifically would you like from each of these situations?

ASSERTION FRAMEWORK

We present a simple yet effective framework for assertiveness that identifies the steps to go through. Clearly it is much easier in theory than in practice. However, we can achieve the goal of personal effectiveness by:

- taking small and manageable steps as outlined in this chapter
- allowing time for consolidation before proceeding to the next stage
- allowing time for regular review and further planning
- persisting!

There are four stages to the framework for assertion. The skills of each stage and the framework can be applied in any context.

- Stage 1 - think it through
- Stage 2 - state what you want or need
- Stage 3 - listen and respond to others
- Stage 4 - negotiate a compromise

We shall firstly apply the framework to specific difficult situations in which we have time to assess the most appropriate approach. Then we shall explore how the framework works in routine or instant situations when we have less time to plan.

DEALING WITH A SPECIFIC PROBLEM

Stage 1: Think it through

Preparation underpins assertion. Because a difficult situation can leave us feeling frustrated,

176

angry or resentful we do not always think clearly. To be assertive we need to diagnose the situation and specific issue, identifying what we want to achieve and how we are going to approach it. If we consider the most important points we wish to make, we will be able to communicate clearly.

What do you really want?

Before we go into a really difficult situation we need to be clear about what we actually want. Sometimes it can help to write it down. Thinking through and isolating the maximum that we want to achieve and the minimum we are prepared to accept gives us the grounding from which to work through compromise (stage 4). We should always ask ourself:

- What do I really want?
- What am I prepared to accept?

Being clear about what we want will help us to ask clearly for it, as we shall see in stage 2.

When is a good time to ask?

Timing is important. It is obviously no good confronting the boss about an unsatisfactory appraisal at 5.00 on a Friday, especially if she's going on holiday. Considering the person's schedule, selecting the most appropriate time of approach and making an appointment if possible will all help.

Choose the place

Obviously it is not always possible to choose the place or environment where we would like to tackle a difficult situation. However, it is worth being aware of the choices we do have. This does not mean rearranging the furniture so that the other person is at a disadvantage (sitting behind a large desk on a high chair is definitely manipulative!). It does mean being aware of the impact of surroundings and compensating for perceived disadvantage with preparation and assertive body language (more on this later in this chapter).

CASE STUDY

Because of her experience, Gabriella had been transferred to manage a new department. To establish herself she wanted to have her team sitting around her in the open plan office. A colleague, at the same grade but with no managerial responsibility, presented a possible problem. She knew she wanted to ask him to move his desk, but felt he might decline.

She decided that rather than ask him in front of the staff it would be easier to ask him in a private office on neutral ground for both of them. The best time to ask would be late in the afternoon so that he could have time overnight to consider where he would like to sit.

EXERCISE –
THINK IT THROUGH

- For any situation in which you would like to be more assertive, think through the best way to tackle it.

- Talking or writing about it can also help.

Stage 2: State what you want or need

'I' statements

When we are going into a difficult situation we need to take full responsibility for what we are saying and doing. If we have done the neccessary planning of stage 1 we will be clear about this. However, we must ensure the message is communicated directly. In assertion, the language is very important and subtle changes to our choice of words will be very significant. If we are behaving assertively there is no hidden agenda.

Using 'I' statements is an essential part of the framework. These are direct statements of our position, actually using the word 'I'. We might be uncomfortable with this, feeling that it conveys an embarrassing focus on ourselves. This is necessary though and it is balanced by our actions in stage 3 when we focus on the other party. The word 'I' forces us to be specific about our position and to take responsibility for it. It is also a useful discipline that makes it difficult for us to lapse into aggression; aggressive statements tend to be 'you' statements.

The 'I' statement tells the other person how we think, feel or view the situation. Compare the following versions:

* *I felt angry when you put me down at that meeting in front of the clients. I would rather you did not do it again.*
* *You made me angry when you put me down at that meeting in front of the clients. Please don't do it again.*

No one has the power to make anyone angry –

although they can try to do so! The second speaker gives away her power and attacks the other person – an aggressive statement. The first speaker is taking responsibility for her own feelings and asking for what she wants. This approach is further illustrated below:

* *I would prefer it if you gave me a specific deadline rather than saying 'as soon as possible'. I have a lot of other work to do. It would help me plan the rest of my workload.*
* *I think the best way forward would be . . .*
* *I believe, from my experience of this sort of situation . . .*
* *I was unhappy when you turned up late and unprepared for the client meeting.*

We disempower ourselves if we use the terms 'you' or 'one' or 'it' when we are talking about ourselves, because we are not fully owning what we are saying or our reaction. Compare the clarity and directness in these example pairs:

> * *When you speak openly about what you think, it is embarrassing.*
> * *I get embarrassed when you speak openly about what you think.*
> * *One ought to give him the benefit of the doubt when he is learning a new skill.*
> * *I feel that I (or we) should give him the benefit of the doubt when he is learning a new skill.*
> * *Managers always have to . . .*
> * *As a manager I have to . . .*

> * *It is impossible to speak to you when you are like this.*
> * *I am finding it impossible to speak to you right now.*

Speaking for oneself, as in the examples, can seem very abrupt and our instinct might be to say that we would find this uncomfortable. Eric and Carol Hall (1988) of the Centre for the Study of Human Relations suggest that 'some of our language habits have developed to make life safe rather than effective'. Just as in changing our behaviour, so changing our habits of speech can seem very artificial. However, assertion is about open, honest and direct communication and we achieve it through the words we choose. The important point is to ask – what do I really mean here?

Ask for what you want

We need to be specific about what we want or do not want at the start, so that the other person is in no doubt about our position or request.

EXERCISE –
SPEAKING FOR YOURSELF

* Practise using 'I' statements to express your views, wishes and opinions.
* Be aware when you avoid doing this.

For example:

* *Thank you for sparing me the time. I would*

like an extra member of staff and these are the reasons why . . .

* *I would like to leave work at 3.00pm today.*
* *I would like you to stop greeting me with a hug. I don't know you that well and I feel uncomfortable.*

Asking for what we want will be more difficult if we are not sure:

* that we are entitled to ask
* that it is acceptable to ask
* of the reaction we might get.

Working on our inner voice and our sense of rights should dispel some of the anxieties. However, women often report that they find it hard to ask for things for themselves.

Another way of looking at this is that sometimes we actually have a responsibility to ask because of our role. We can perceive of asking as a personal favour when in fact it is essential for our job. For example, asking for help with a project we are having difficulties with is our responsibility, as is asking a team member to tackle a task that has to be done or to correct an error.

EXERCISE –
ASKING FOR WHAT YOU WANT

* Identify things that you would like to ask for but have difficulty in asking.

Be direct and to the point

Speaking directly and to the point demands that

we express our position succinctly. If we waffle because we would rather not say it at all, or ramble because we have not thought it through, we might as well not say it at all.

* *I'm terribly sorry to be a nuisance and I know you're ever so busy but I wondered if you had the time . . .*

Direct statements

- avoid padding
- avoid preamble
- come to the point

CASE STUDY

Gabriella knew how she wanted the office to be rearranged, but she felt anxious because John could be quite difficult. He did not like change and she believed he did not particularly like her.

For her own benefit she had written out what she wanted and the reasons for needing it so that she would not waste time. She mentally prepared herself by reminding herself of her right to ask him and the fact that what she was asking was not unreasonable, as it was to benefit the department.

She started out by saying: 'John, thank you for agreeing to see me here. I would like to talk to you about rearranging the desks, as I would like to have my immediate team sitting around me. This would mean that you would have to move from your current position.'

EXERCISE – DIRECT COMMUNICATION

- For a specific, personally relevant situation, write a statement of what you want or need that has no padding or preamble

- Then try making the statement.

Stage 3: Listen and respond to others

An important difference between assertion and aggression is the response to the other person. Our behaviour could be read as aggressive unless we take into consideration the feelings and situation of the other person. In order to do this effectively we need to listen, observe the other person and make empathetic statements.

Listen

At the heart of assertion is the skill of listening. This is important as it enables us to find out the other person's views and show our respect for them in a practical way.

Effective listening involves:

- giving them our full attention and not trying to do something else at the same time
- showing we are listening by our non-verbal communication
- clarifying our understanding by summarising their main points

It allows us to appreciate their position fully and clarify any areas of misunderstanding. Many disagreements can be resolved quite simply once both parties are clear about the other person's view.

Listening helps the process because:

- it communicates our respect for the other person's feelings, wishes, opinions and rights even though we may not agree with them
- it allows a balance in the interaction between their views and ours
- it influences their perception of us
- a positive outcome is difficult without it

EXERCISE – LISTENING

- When you are listening to someone, identify any distractions – including your own inner voice – that interfere with your hearing the message.
- Work at concentrating on what they are saying so that you hear all that they say.

Observe the other person

If we are to respond to the other person rather than react to the behaviour, we need to observe the whole picture. Assertiveness demands observation of the non-verbal behaviour of the person, awareness of our preferred automatic reaction to the emotional dimension of the message and a decision regarding our behaviour in response.

The non-verbal behaviour, including their vocal tone, can give us additional problems – or insights. Do their words and non-verbal communication match? Are we hearing what is implied rather than what is stated? This can be a particular problem in response to manipulative behaviour when we pick up the nuances and lose sight of the words, which of course hinders our own verbal response. As a rule it is best to respond to what is said and not to what is implied.

Perceived conflict between what is said and how it is said can also guide our further response. We may:

- attempt to clarify their position
- make a mental note to check in the future
- feel more confident ourselves

EXERCISE – OBSERVATION SKILLS

- Develop your observation skills by observing people generally.
- Note your reaction to their non-verbal communication.

Make empathic statements

True empathy demands that we really try to see the situation from the other person's point of view – and show that we are doing so. It is an extension of listening and is best conveyed by a playing back of their main points. The words used are important, as it is easy to patronise people with stock phrases that give the impression that you are merely using a set of artificial techniques. The following clichés can be counterproductive:

* *I hear where you are coming from.*
* *I understand your point of view.*
* *I hear what you say.*

In order to be empathic we must:

- listen
- explain what we understand their position to be
- include reference to the fact that we can appreciate or understand it
- separate this from our own position
- return to our 'I statements'

In some circumstances it will be necessary to give a response that is counter to the other's position. For example:

* *I appreciate the fact that you want an increase in salary, especially as you haven't had an increase for over a year. However, because of the recession and the financial difficulties experienced by the company we are unable to give you one at the present time.*

187

Empathy aims to communicate that the person has been heard and their position at least acknowledged. Even though they may not get what they want, respect is thus shown.

CASE STUDY

Gabriella told John that she would like him to move his desk, so that she could have her team sitting around her. She told him, 'It will make communication, monitoring of work and problem-solving a lot easier. It's going to take time for me to get to know them, so I would really appreciate your support in this matter. What do you think?'

John listened to what Gabriella had to say and responded by saying. 'Look, this rearrangement might suit you but it's going to be really inconvenient for me. I need to have access to the computer and I work with a couple of your team on certain projects. To be quite honest I'm not happy about your plans at all.'

Gabriella could see that John was annoyed at the thought of having to move and said, 'John I didn't realise that you would feel quite so strongly about moving your desk. I haven't laid down any plans in tablets of stone, perhaps we could discuss a way forward.'

EXERCISE – LISTENING AND EMPATHISING

- Practise reflecting in your own words the main points that others make to you to show you have been listening and to check your understanding.

- Summarising a longer statement can also help assertive communication.

188

Stage 4: Negotiate a compromise

An essential element of the process is negotiating to find a middle ground for both parties. This can be achieved only if we have completed the first three stages: we cannot negotiate effectively unless we are clear about what we want and we have listened to the other person's point of view. It is only when both parties have been honest that a compromise can be negotiated.

If we bear in mind the importance of clear 'I' statements and empathy we will display the necessary skills. It may well be quite a slow process and sometimes thinking time needs to be incorporated. The objective is an outcome that at least partially satisfies everyone.

CASE STUDY

Gabriella could understand why John found it convenient to stay in his current place. However, she still needed to change the office round so that she could do her job more effectively. She said to him, 'John, my understanding from you is that you need access to the computer and you are working with a couple of the team, Karen and David, on some specific projects. Is that correct?' 'Yes,' John replied.

Gabriella proposed, 'Well, what if we look at the seating arrangements to ensure that you have your needs met, but I also have the team sitting round me. I'm sure this is possible. Would you be prepared to look at an alternative arrangement encompassing both of our requirements.'

John responded by saying, 'I am willing to look at something if I can have my requirements fulfilled. Can we think about this overnight and talk tomorrow morning?'

When negotiating for compromise:

- repeatedly work through stages 2 and 3
- express willingness to reach a solution
- explore what each party can offer
- think creatively
- state the compromise clearly when it is reached

Putting it all together

Sasha had started a new job as administration manager in a blue chip company. The previous post holder had not been taken very seriously by senior managers and was virtually unknown to the other regional offices throughout the UK.

Her new boss, who had also just started with the company, wanted to raise the profile of the department and had been very specific about this at her interview. Sasha recognised that if she administered the company profit share scheme through the regional offices she would get herself and the department on the company map. In order to achieve this it would mean contackling the Salary Administration Manager, who administered the scheme centrally and was notorious for blocking any changes that might threaten her own power base.

Sasha decided to write down the advantages to the members of staff and to the Salary Administration Manager if she took over the scheme. Over a period of a couple of weeks she gathered all the facts and figures she would require and put her case initially in a memo.

When the Salary Administration Manager phoned up Sasha was very clear in her mind about what she wanted and the reasons. She restated her case and listened to her colleague's objections. She told her she understood her objections, but that her plan would take greater care of all the staff as individuals, as it would be administered by regionally based representatives who would be assisted by her on a regular basis. The existing format for the scheme meant none of the staff knew the Salary Admininistration Manager. If they missed out on their share entitlement and found out, the company had to spend additional funds compensating them.

Sasha stated clearly what she wanted and said her case was beneficial to all. As a compromise she agreed to let the Salary Administration Manager know how the scheme was proceeding and to send her copies of all the paperwork. By being very clear about what she wanted Sasha achieved her objective.

Changing our behaviour is not easy, especially if we have spent a life-time dealing with specific situations in a certain way. The good news is that, by making the decision to apply the framework for assertion and practising sufficiently, our practised behaviour will eventually become our natural behaviour. Learning to be assertive is no different from learning any other skill such as playing an instrument or driving a car; the more we practise the easier it is and the more accomplished we become. This is illustrated in the following fairy story.

The Criminal and the Princess

Once upon a time there was a beautiful Chinese princess who wanted to find a husband. She was very clear about the kind of husband she wanted. He must be kind, thoughtful, generous, patient and honest. The description was sent throughout the land.

An evil, ugly criminal heard about the princess's request. He thought this was too good an opportunity to miss, so he had a beautiful mask made of a face that was kind, thoughtful, generous, patient and honest. The evil criminal presented himself with the mask to the beautiful princess. When the princess met him, she was so enamoured she decided to become engaged to him and that they would marry in a year's time.

The evil criminal wore the mask and had to 'act as if' he was kind, thoughtful, generous, patient and honest. When the year had ended the criminal felt deeply ashamed and told the princess the truth about himself and what he had done. The princess was deeply distressed and ordered him to take off the mask. When the criminal took off the mask he had a handsome kind face. The princess exclaimed, 'Why have you gone to such trouble to disguise your face, when it is exactly the same as the mask?'

Source: Adaptation reprinted from the Book *Lifeline Sampler*, copyright 1985, by permission of Overeaters Anonymous Inc., World Service Office, Rio Rancho, New Mexico, USA.

By 'acting as if' we are assertive we will eventually become it over a period of time. The situations that cause us problems will not go away.

However, by applying the assertion framework on a regular basis, we will no longer have to think through how to respond assertively – we will do it automatically.

ROUTINE USE OF THE FRAMEWORK

Becoming naturally assertive in difficult situations takes time, and during the learning process we may need to develop some fast reactions to cope on the spot and give ourselves time to think through our response.

* I'd like time to think about what you've said. I'll get back to you [when.]
* I'm not sure about that. Are you saying [summarise the main points]?
* I've got a lot on my plate at the moment. I'll take your request into consideration and get back to you.
* I'm not clear about what you've said. Could you repeat it.
* That's an interesting observation. I hadn't thought of it like that.
* Could you say more?
* I don't remember agreeing to that point. I need to refer back to my notes and let you know.

The non-verbal impact

Our body language, appearance and use of voice can reinforce or contradict our meaning. In any situation we need to be aware of non-verbal leakage – that is the gestures and mannerisms that can detract from what we are trying to say.

193

Given that up to 90% of any message can be conveyed through our voice and body we must pay attention to this aspect of our personal presentation.

Smiling

Through our conditioning we may have been taught to smile at all times as it conveys warmth and rapport to the other person. This would be highly inappropriate in those situations where we need to convey concern, unhappiness or seriousness, for example when disciplining a member of staff. Constant smiles can be interpreted as nervousness, shyness or a need to be liked.

Eye contact

Appropriate eye contact creates the most effective impression. Too much or too intense eye contact could be read as aggression or, depending on the situation, a sexual overture. Insufficient eye contact may suggest lack of attention, lack of confidence or submission.

Looking at any point on the face in the area bordered by the outer ends of the eyebrows and the tip of the nose can help those who feel uncomfortable with direct eye contact, and breaking the gaze from time to time is natural provided we do not look all around the room or at our watch and so signify boredom! A practical tip for those times we need to asssert ourselves more strongly is to hold eye contact a few moments longer than the norm.

Mannerisms

Mannerisms act as an indicator of feeling.

Common mannerisms when feeling un-comfortable are twiddling with a piece of hair, fiddling with an earring, bracelet or pen, covering the mouth with a hand, and these can detract from the impression of confidence. It is helpful to increase awareness of our common mannerisms; one way is to ask the people we trust and who know us well what particular gestures we display and to aim to minimise those that undermine us or our message.

Posture, movement and use of space

How we use our body in a confrontational situation will be significant. Leaning forward can appear aggressive; shrinking back indicates that we are passive. When standing, the distance we take from the person will have an impact on our power.

Jane

Jane was representing her organisation at a large meeting of other charities' representatives. She was putting forward a campaigning proposal for a new scheme involving them all.

Sitting alongside her was a woman with a predominantly aggressive style who spoke very strongly about why Jane's organisation should not take the leading role in this project. As Jane felt herself slide down the chair in fear she realised that the woman was undermining her in front the others.

Immediately sitting upright she smiled at the group, acknowledged the point the other woman was making and then put forward her case again with conviction, reinforced by her assertive body language and voice. She won her case.

If we want to deal assertively with someone it is best to be at the same eye level. Many women find that taller men and women use their height as a form of intimidation, so suggesting to the person that you should both sit down can help ease an awkward confrontation. If the person is angry, the change in stance can help defuse the situation.

In some circumstances it is appropriate to stage-manage any scene we can control – with subtlety – to help equalise the power. Aspects of the physical surrounding to take into account are:

- the physical level of both parties – height conveys power
- the person whose territory it is will tend to have the edge on power
- furniture can – form a barrier
                 – create or reinforce a sense of status
                 – be uncomfortable
- sun or bright light from a window affects the interaction:
  - looking into bright light can be distracting
  - eyes tend to gravitate towards us if we are in front of a window
  - the face of someone sitting in front of a sunny window will not be so clearly seen

Louise

Louise felt intimidated by some of her colleagues. She found that if they were annoyed or had a complaint they would storm into her office and come up behind her. As her desk was against the wall, which she faced, she was at an immediate disadvantage as they would tower over her from behind her chair. When she moved the desk away from the wall and sat behind it, she could see her colleagues coming in and could invite them to sit down at her level – defusing some of the tension!

Dress

Our dress and physical appearance will contribute to the total message we convey. Dressing according to the image we wish to present is another dimension of communicating personal power. The choices we make say a great deal about how we view ourselves. This is not about how much money we spend on our wardrobe – it is about how much care we take with our appearance.

---

* 'When I didn't have any money I made sure I had a really good haircut to communicate that I do take care of myself.'
* 'I can't afford expensive clothes, but I will save up for good-quality accessories.'
* 'Investment in a good-quality suit made me feel more positive and professional.'
* 'I find that certain clothes give me more confidence.'
* 'As I work long hours I plan my clothes a week ahead so that I can forget about what to wear.'
* 'I find that second-hand shops have an impressive range of good-quality clothes that I could not otherwise afford.'
* 'Like it or not, people do make judgements about us based on how seriously we take our grooming.'

Many women find the subject of dressing for work complex as there are so many possibilities. For men the 'rules' are generally much clearer. This does though give us great opportunities to present ourselves as individuals and use our image positively. It also presents more opportunities for mistakes.

It is helpful to consider:

- the culture of the organisation and formal or informal dress codes
- what other women wear at different internal levels organisationally
- do we dress at our level or at another level?
- do we want to stand out or merge in?
- what statement(s) we are wishing to make with our appearance

Nicola Whitmarsh, freelance image consultant, says:

Some women have a tendency to dress in a masculine style, with the hard navy blue or pinstripe suit and the severe white blouse buttoned up at the collar. The key is to dress professionally and look your best as a woman. This means avoid baring any flesh, as the more you expose the less seriously people will take you.

Professional dressing is all about our grooming and the small details. If you can't wear nail varnish without chipping it, then don't wear it. Always have clean, tidy, well-cut hair. Carry a spare pair of tights. Use a good-quality pen, rather than one with the end chewed off. Invest in a smart-looking handbag. Think about what your shoes say about you and are they clean and comfortable. Obviously people take in the whole picture, but on first meeting they also home in on the small details, which can undermine the overall impact.

Jackets denote authority. If a tailored jacket does not suit your personal image or culture, there is a wide range of softer-silhouette jackets. Apart from giving a more professional image, they are also useful for finishing off an outfit.

People in our culture can feel threatened by well-dressed women, as if it's a bit suspect that we should present ourselves positively. We need to rise above people's attitudes and dress well for ourselves. Before going for an interview for a new job it's worth checking out the image people project in the organisation if we can, so we may blend in with the culture but stand out with a sense of style.

Think about the message you want to project in a meeting or formal presentation. Dark colours, such as black, navy blue and grey, represent authority, which is enhanced by contrast with a light blouse. Taupe, beige and pale colours are the listening colours, encouraging people to open up more easily. Red is dramatic and represents power. It's a good colour if you want to stand out, but not if you want people to confide in you. Before you go anywhere think about what you are going to say and do, and the impression you want to leave in people's minds. Colours and clothing are a tool that can make or break your overall impression.

There is more on image in Chapter 7.

Disempowering language

Just as our body language is critical to the impact we create, so our tone of voice and the actual words we choose can detract from our message of power.

Avoiding statements

Asking a question when we are really making a statement reduces our impact. It is a classic example of not really saying what we want to and so not getting heard.

* *Do you want to go to the pictures?*
* *I would like to go to the pictures. Would you like to come too?*
* *Would you do this for me?*
* *I'd like you to do this for me please.*

Habitually asking instead of stating can erode our sense of personal power because it is a way of not taking responsibility. It creates the impression that others have the power to choose or are doing us favours. Of course, asking questions when that is what we intend is essential.

Ending with a question

Concluding a presentation or statement of opinion with a question erodes the case we have just put forward. The question suggests we are looking for approval, rather than believing in what we have said.

* *I believe this approach might work well – what do you think?*

Raised intonation at the end of sentences

Sometimes we speak as if we are asking when in fact we are making a statement. We raise our intonation as if there is a question mark at the end and so imply hesitancy in our ideas that needs a response by way of confirmation. Lowering intonation at the end of a sentence can suggest a more definite and confident stance.

Personal put-downs

Introductory statements such as:

*   *I know this is a silly question . . .*
*   *I've probably missed the point but . . .*

are ways we undermine our position and our power. By putting ourselves and what we say down we are reinforcing a possible view that we lack credibility. This will have an impact on our own sense of self-worth in the long term.

Being overly apologetic

Excessively polite speech, such as the exaggerated use of 'please', 'thank you' and 'sorry', can imply we are apologising or grateful for existing. Saying it once is enough. The habit of preceding any disagreement, refusal of a request or indeed statement with 'sorry' also suggests that we have no right to make our view known.

Vagueness

Qualifying expressions such as:

*   *sort of*
*   *you know*

* *do you know what I mean?*
* *I could be wrong*

can make us sound uncommitted, lacking in real conviction or not definite. Words like 'hope' or 'try' if overused convey a lack of confidence and an indefinite approach. Compare:

* *I'll try to finish that proposal this evening.*

with

* *I will give you the proposal at 10.00 tomorrow.*

'However' or 'but'

'But' can be perceived as an aggressive, defensive word in a sentence, whereas 'however' is a linking word. For example:

* *I would prefer to start at 8.30pm; however, if this is going to cause great inconvenience I will make arrangements to come in at 8.00am*

is more positive than

* *I would prefer to finish at 5.00pm, but if it's going to cause a lot of problems I'll finish off at 5.30pm.*

As a general rule, 'however' is used instead of 'but' as it links the ideas instead of expressing them as opposites.

DEALING WITH ASSERTIVE BEHAVIOUR

If both parties are behaving assertively it should be easier to communicate effectively as they will:

- be listening
- be acting from a basis of mutual respect
- be clear and direct
- not be playing power games
- have no hidden agendas.

Clearly we will not always agree with each other and we may need to agree to differ, or to defer discussion to a later date after further thinking time. Communication that reaches stalemate or leaves us feeling there is a breakdown suggests that one party is not fully listening to the other or that there is no willingness to shift ground or move on. We can check our own behaviour and practise our skills, yet we cannot expect that every difficulty will be resolved.

Assertiveness is a constant process of learning by doing without the belief that we can control all the outcomes. We can only do our best. In Chapter 6 we explore ways of dealing with difficult people and situations whilst maintaining our personal power.

SUMMARY – PRACTICAL TIPS

* Recognise the behaviour of the other person before responding
* Do not give away personal power by reacting to the person, but choose your response
* Act as if you are assertive, even if you do not feel it at the time

* *Think through difficult situations in terms of:*
  – *what do I want?*
  – *when is a good time to ask?*
  – *where is the most appropriate place?*
* *Use 'I' statements*
* *Be clear, direct and specific in your statements*
* *Observe, listen and empathise with the other person*
* *Negotiate a compromise*
* *Ensure your body language and tone of voice are congruent with your words*
* *Avoid disempowering language*

PART III

EMPOWERMENT AT WORK

6

MAINTAINING PERSONAL POWER

Life is not the way it's supposed to be. It's the way it is. The way you cope with it is what makes the difference.
(Virginia Satir)

We can expect to experience difficult situations at work. Our capacity for handling them effectively may well influence:

- our long-term relationships with our manager
- our ability to manage our staff
- effective working relationships with colleagues
- our ability to get the best resources
- our dealings with suppliers and customers
- the achievement of our job objectives
- our promotability

Without practical approaches to tough decisions, the increased stress levels can leave us feeling disempowered. In this chapter we look at a range of techniques that will help us to maintain personal power in difficult times.

207

> * 'Disciplining a member of staff was the hardest thing I've had to do. However, it sorted out a serious ongoing problem and sent a strong signal to other members of staff.'
> * 'My colleagues were always late for meetings – they seemed to think I didn't mind because I never spoke up, but I was furious. When I initially raised the matter they were surprised – but they stopped arriving late.'
> * 'My boss seemed to think it was perfectly acceptable to bawl me out in front of the rest of the department. Confronting him about it was extremely hard, but he doesn't do it anymore.'
> * 'When I finally plucked up the courage to speak up at meetings, I felt as if I was interrupted all the time. It only stopped when I spoke up more strongly – they hadn't realised they were doing it.'

BEING RESPECTED IS MORE IMPORTANT THAN BEING LIKED

A difficult barrier that many of us have to confront is our desire to be liked. Whilst this is a natural desire, as a driving force it is incompatible with the role of manager, with being credible at work or with leading our lives as fully functioning adults.

A desire to be liked leads us to run the risk of compromising ourself, our position or the organisation. However we behave, we cannot control whether people do like us and if it is our main concern we open ourselves up to manipulation.

Effectiveness at work can demand we make hard decisions and implement others' hard decisions. If we are responsible for the performance of others we need to let them know where they stand. Raising concerns about others' behaviour or expressing our feelings may well be necessary if we are to confront problems. Whilst concern for individuals is important, over-concern for their responses to us as a person may prevent a clear understanding of the implications of our actions. We will need to deal with circumstances from an objective perspective, unhampered by ego. Ensuring we are clear about what is acceptable and unacceptable behaviour can help us to tackle the really tough moments.

It is more powerful to act from a sense of personal values: a code that gives us personal respect and that is more likely to gain us the respect of others. Even if it does not, we will have won personal approval.

FEEDBACK

The giving and receiving of feedback is a powerful aid to development and change. We cannot change our actions if we are unaware of their impact. Feedback can lead to:

- improvements in performance
- modification of behaviour
- increased motivation
- enhanced communication and better relationships

In essence, giving feedback involves taking a specific situation and offering the person or people involved our response to their behaviour. This may include a description of the behaviour as we saw it and the effect it has had on us – our reaction to it. We receive feedback when we hear from others how they see us and our actions. We can then act on these perceptions if we choose.

The balance between positive and negative feedback will be dependent on the culture of the organisation and the personal preference of the individual. It will affect morale and performance and thus is an important part of the managing process if we want to empower others.

> *   *'I've worked in the company for six months and I haven't been told any- thing so I assume it's all okay.'*
> *   *'I am given heaps of praise for every- thing I organise. This also applies to peo- ple who I know do not perform well, so I never really know how I'm doing.'*
> *   *'My boss gives me regular feedback in my one-to-one meetings. We focus on three areas: where I am doing well, where I can improve and what I should be working on next. I come out feeling really motivated because I can trust her to develop me and help me learn.'*

Sometimes it is necessary to give negative feed-back to the people we manage. The following guidelines help the giving of criticism to be positive. They all expand on the assertive approach outlined in Chapter 5.

Check the motive

Sometimes feedback is used as punishment. Giving criticism to the individual in order to put them down does not help them develop and is not in keeping with an empowering approach.

Be specific

It is not helpful to an individual to criticise obliquely or in an unspecific way; commenting on attitude, for example, could mean they are late for work, they do not participate at meetings, they dress inappropriately or they do not check their letters before sending them out. If we want to help a person move forward, we need to collect the facts, identify exactly what we are criticising and be clear about the areas that need to be tackled.

Criticise the behaviour and not the person

Dealing with the specific behaviour that needs to be addressed and avoiding statements about general character is good practice. It would not be helpful to say:

*   *You're hopeless the way you always turn up late.*

211

A more assertive approach would be:

* *I would like to bring to your attention that you have arrived at 9.30am for the last four days. The starting time is 9.00am. Is there any particular reason for this?*

Be clear about what you want

The person can change effectively only if we give them clear guidelines on exactly what is required of them in future and the reason for the need to change.

* *Overall the presentation was very good. However, I'd like you to get the overheads presented in colour and with our logo on it. It looks more professional.*

Use 'I' statements

If we are telling the person how we feel or see a situation we need to take responsibility for our perception and use 'I' statements rather than hiding behind 'we' or 'one'.

Listen to what the person has to say

There are many good reasons why someone has not fulfilled our expectations. An important part of the assertion process is to hear how they feel and their reasons for their behaviour. Summarising what they have said to check understanding demonstrates that we have really listened.

*   *So what you are saying is that since you have moved house you have had real difficulties with your journey to work and this is the reason why you're late in. I can really understand the problems; however . . .*

Keep to the subject

If we are clear from the start why we are giving the criticism it is easier not to be distracted. It enables us to avoid getting into an argument about other issues and to deal with one issue at a time.

*   *'I am concerned about the three complaints we've had from customers in the last week about late delivery.'*
   'But we're really busy and you didn't tell us about the new product launch.'
   'Perhaps we could discuss that later. Right now I'd like to discuss the complaints and how we can prevent them in future.'

Stay calm and neutral

A calm voice and neutral, relaxed body language help both parties. Being clear about our motive for giving the criticism can have an effect on the non-verbal impression we give to the person.

Sarah

Justina had recently joined Sarah's department and was settling in reasonably well. However, she suffered from a personal hygiene problem which had been brought to Sarah's attention. She was concerned for Justina as members of staff were beginning to make unkind comments about her behind her back.

213

Although Justina seemed unaware of the comments, Sarah knew it was her responsibility as a manager to raise the matter.

She called Justina into her office and said to her, 'How are you settling in?' Justina replied, 'I'm really enjoying the work, and the people are friendly enough, but it's going to take a while.'

Sarah said, 'I feel awkward having to do this, however I feel that if I had this problem I would want to know. I have been conscious for the last three weeks that you seem to have a personal hygiene problem. I would like you to do something about it.' Justina was obviously very embarrassed and said, 'I don't know what to say. I'm absolutely mortified. Has every-one been discussing it?' Sarah was equally embarrassed, 'I can't comment on what the other team members have said. I can understand your reaction.'

EXERCISE –
GIVING CRITICISM

- Think of criticism that you would like to give or need to give.

- Using the guidelines above, work out what and how you will say it. You might find it useful to rehearse it with a friend.

- Then do the real thing!

RECEIVING CRITICISM

Just as we may find it difficult to give criticism, people may find it hard to give it to us. Although we may be resistant to hearing it or respond defensively, criticism or feedback can be extremely useful in raising our level of perform-ance. A positive attitude on our part and a calm, reasonable and constructive approach by the person giving the criticism can lead to helpful, regular feedback and a mature relationship.

Sometimes, of course, criticism is not given well; it can be accompanied by put-downs or, when we seek further information, the points are withdrawn or it turns into a personal attack. In these circumstances, maintaining our asser-tive body language and working calmly through the framework will help us come out of the encounter in the most positive way possible.

As with giving criticism, assertion principles can be applied very simply when dealing with criticism that is given to us.

Listen carefully

Awareness of any initial resistance we may feel is the first step. Before we respond to the other person we must listen intently to what they are saying. It will be hard to do so if our inner voice is saying that it isn't fair or that they are wrong. Quietening any internal self-defence, focusing on what is being said and showing we are listen-ing with attentive non-verbal communication will help begin the process.

Check understanding

Part of effective listening is to check under-standing. We might want to clarify any of these points:

- What exactly are they criticising – is it something we have done or is the criticism of us as a person?

  * *You always make such a mess of any project I hand to you. You waste all our time because I have to pick up the pieces. You really let me down.*

If we suspect the criticism is general and personal it is hard to proceed. If, after working through the points below, we still feel that it is a personal attack, we may choose to challenge it.

- Is the criticism specific or vague?
- Is it clear or unclear?
  If the criticism is unclear or vague we must ask for clarification, more specific information and perhaps examples of the problem area.

  * *So you believe the proposal was sloppy in its content – can you please be more specific. Which parts exactly? Can you explain what you mean and give me some examples?*

- Are there any pointers on how we can improve?
  Having heard the criticism we may need help in addressing the problem. Asking for practical ideas shows a positive attitude.

  * *I understand that you are not happy with the way I dealt with the disciplinary problem in my team. Could you advise me on how I should have tackled it?*

- In our view is the criticism justified or unjustified?

  Despite detail and example, we might disagree with the criticism.

Unjustified criticism

If the criticism is wholly unjustified, repeating it back in our own words shows that we have understood the other person's views. Then we need to tell them why we think their perception of the situation is incorrect.

* *I understand that you believe I should not have suspended him from work. However, I spent a long time collecting information about his performance and the situation was getting out of hand. Smashing the car on company business with the witnesses saying he was in the wrong was the final straw.*

If part of the criticism is justified we can state this and address that particular area of concern.

Justified criticism

If the criticism is wholly justified we should:

- admit it immediately
- apologise once

By accepting the criticism graciously we can remedy the situation. We are also showing greater dignity than if we over-apologise, ask for forgiveness or deny it. We can also:

217

- ask for guidance on how to improve
- offer to resolve the problem if appropriate

Use 'I' statements

'I' statements when receiving criticism demonstrate that we are taking responsibility for our reaction and opinion.

* *I am concerned to hear you say that.*
* *I agree that I did rush that last piece of work. However, I do usually take great care and disagree with your view that I am always careless.*
* *I accept that I made a mistake and am sorry about the time it took to rectify the problem.*

Ask for thinking time

If we are shocked, distressed or confused by the criticism it is worth asking for the time to think about what the person has said before responding to it. This can buy us the time to calm down if we feel very strongly about the matter and help prevent an over-reaction, which could seriously undermine our credibility.

* *My line manager has made no mention of any problem with my performance. I am shocked that you are saying the directors think there are serious problems with my department. I would like some time to think about what you've just said before responding.*

Responding to implied criticism

People sometimes hint at criticism without stating it clearly. This is a common manipulative

ploy and can undermine us subtly. Responding
to the implication – often conveyed through the
non-verbal messages – can leave us feeling confused if the meaning is denied.

As a rule, responding only to what is stated
and not to what is implied maintains our power.
We might seek clarification of their position but
will not react to hints without checking them
out.

* *That was a great piece of work. (Said with a
  sarcastic sneer)*

We could respond:

* *Thank you. I'm glad you were pleased.*

or

* *You don't sound too pleased. What did you
  really think of the work?*

Reading criticism where none is meant

If our confidence is low we may read criticism
where none is intended. If we are aware of this
as a pattern it is vital to stop the automatic
reaction. There are suggestions on how to do
this in Chapter 4. Seeking regular feedback on
our performance and acting on the information
will also help us improve our performance as
well as our self-esteem.

Giving and receiving compliments

The flip side of criticism is the giving and receiving of compliments and praise. A common

response to positive feedback is embarrassment. We might feel that we should do the job well as that is what we are paid for or that everyone can do this particular thing just as well. These attitudes are undermining, not only for ourselves but also for the person giving the praise. By denying their perception we in effect put them down under the guise of modesty. Learning to accept compliments effectively balances the learning from criticism. To accept a compliment, all we need to do is smile at the person and say 'thank you'.

<u>EXERCISE–</u>
<u>RECEIVING FEEDBACK</u>

- At the next opportunity, be aware of your response to feedback, both positive and negative, and practise receiving it assertively.

THE BENEFITS OF REGULAR FEEDBACK

Giving and receiving feedback – both positive and negative – are essential parts of any manager's skill repertoire. Establishing regular one-to-one meetings for performance review with our staff and our immediate boss gives people the opportunity to address problems at an early stage and can avoid misunderstandings or major resentments at the review or appraisal time. Regular feedback helps create an atmosphere where people can communicate openly, as they know issues will be dealt with in a responsible and mature fashion, ultimately improving job performance and teamwork, and enhancing working relationships.

> ### EXERCISE– REGULAR FEEDBACK
>
> - Establish a pattern of giving and receiving regular feedback with your colleagues.

DEALING WITH DISCIPLINARY MATTERS

Women – and men – often avoid dealing with discipline problems because they fear the repercussions. Concerns may include:

- potential conflict
- not being liked
- getting it wrong

Not addressing the problem at the time can result in its aggravation. The responsibility to tackle difficult situations is implicit in the role of managing others, although it can be very hard to do.

THE PURPOSE OF DISCIPLINARY ACTION

The aim of disciplining a member of staff is to inform them of unacceptable behaviour or performance, and to correct it by establishing an understanding of the required standard and giving guidance to the person so they can achieve the standard. The objective is to help someone improve, not to remove them. It is essential to

221

identify the reasons for the drop in job performance or conduct through sensitive counselling
and then to use coaching or training to address
the problem. Careful monitoring of the individual is essential.

To avoid serious legal repercussions, it is
absolutely essential to involve personnel professionals when considering implementing the
organisation's disciplinary procedure. If access
to a personnel professional is not possible, follow the organisation's disciplinary procedure
precisely, and obtain and read the ACAS handbook *Discipline at Work (1987).* Each disciplinary situation will be individual and will require
complex consideration to protect the interests of
all parties involved in the process.

EXERCISE–
DISCIPLINE PROCEDURE

- Always check with your personnel
  department for advice and guidance
  first.

- Check your organisation's disciplinary
  procedure.

- Be prepared to use it if necessary.

- If you do not have a personnel department, research the legal and ACAS procedure thoroughly.

CONFRONTING DIFFICULT ISSUES

Wanting harmonious relationships can mean
we avoid confronting difficult issues or others'

problem behaviour. However, by not addressing a problem and allowing it to continue, we erode our personal power.

Sometimes, tackling a tough situation head on is the most effective way of dealing with it. We can be clearer of the way forward by asking ourselves:

- What would be the benefit to me and the other person if I tackle this issue?
- What is the worst thing that could happen?

Many women find it difficult to express their more negative emotions to others, especially irritation, anger or feeling upset. Our conditioning has often taught us that nice girls do not get angry and that we certainly do not state our feelings or confront other people. An assertive approach enables us to express these feelings, thoughts and opinions without becoming inappropriately over-emotional or losing control.

SAYING 'NO'

We will quite often want to say 'yes' to requests. However, if we always find ourselves saying 'yes' when we want to say 'no' – and regretting it – we will need to develop the technique of saying 'no'. This is an important assertion skill that helps us claim personal power by:

- preventing us from becoming overloaded with work or bombarded by other people's problems
- enabling us to manage our time more effectively and thus helping to reduce our stress levels

- helping us to maintain the boundaries between us and others

Our most fundamental rights as human beings include the right to ask for what we want and the right to say 'no'; the two go hand in hand.

Many women find it very difficult to say 'no' because of fear of the other person's reaction and the desire to be liked and accepted. Wanting to help can lead us to consider the consequences for the other person rather than the practical ones based on our limitations. If we are not used to refusing requests we can feel guilty about putting our own position first.

Another way to look at it is to consider how, by saying 'yes', we are actually meeting our own needs. For example:

* *I will be thought of as indispensable.*
* *It can excuse me from doing something else.*
* *I'll be the centre of attention.*
* *People will think I'm really helpful.*
* *I can ask for favours in return.*
* *I can be seen positively by everyone.*

Just as it is easy to confuse the request with the person, so we can think that saying 'yes' generates a kind of emotional currency that keeps our account in credit.

We might also say 'yes' because we assume that the other person will be upset or hurt if we say 'no'. The assumption may of course be wrong and we could create further problems for the other person by complying. Questioning and perhaps challenging our asssumptions about the other person's reaction can prove in-sightful.

Pippa

Pippa works as a personnel officer in an engineering company. The company was going through a period of restructuring. She was involved in the preparation to make people redundant and in interviewing people for newly created posts. 'I was being pulled in both directions. I had two senior managers who wanted me to sort out the figures, look at the costs and organise the announcements for the redundancies for them. I had another three managers wanting me to carry out the inter-viewing with them for the new posts. All the interviews had been scheduled over two days and had taken quite a long time to arrange.

Normally I would have carried out the interviews and worked on the redundancies by coming in really early and staying very late out of fear of disrupting the managers. This time I decided if I wanted to be effective in the interviewing process I would have to stand my ground and say 'no' to them. They were really resentful to begin with, but I gave them my explanation. There was nothing they could do. I wasn't being difficult. I was ensur-ing that I would be in a fit state for the interviews. It worked out well in the end.'

Saying what we mean and choosing what to say are important steps to maintaining personal power. When we choose to say 'no' it is effective to use the following framework:

- Use 'I' statements and if necessary tell the person how you feel
  * *I feel awkward saying this.*
  * *I am unhappy to disappoint you.*
- Include the word 'no' in your response
- Give explanations not excuses

- Show understanding of their situation
- Offer an alternative or suggest a compromise if you can
- Apologise once, if it is appropriate, but not profusely. Be specific about what you are apologising for.
- Do not apologise for asserting your right to refuse.
- Speak calmly and slowly and look the person in the eye.

Bianca

Bianca's company was spread over three sites within a 20 mile radius. A reorganisation led to the closing down of two sites and relocation of staff to head office. This meant that a number of people would have problems getting to work unless they had their own transport. Bianca's colleague Robert asked her if she would give him a lift to and from work.

Robert: 'Bianca, as we've all got to go to the head office site and I haven't got transport could you give me a lift to and from work? I will pay you petrol money.'

Bianca: 'Robert, I feel uncomfortable saying this, however I am going to say 'no'. Your home isn't far from mine I know, but we work slightly different hours and I have to leave exactly on time to be home for my children. I would not like the commitment. I know it is an awkward journey and there are quite a number of you. Have you not thought about asking the company to lay on some transport? I heard some of the others talking about it'

Robert: 'I didn't know about that. Can't you give me a lift until it gets started?'

Bianca: 'I'm willing to help in the short term; however, as I explained, I do have commitments to my family and cannot change those arrangements. If you are ready to travel when I do then you can have a lift until you arrange something else. Can we set a limit on how long that will be?'

MUDDLE AND CONFUSION

On the occasions we feel we are receiving mixed messages, are unclear of what is expected of us or are muddled about our work priorities, discrepancy assertion is a useful technique. It involves pointing out two contradictory messages and asking for clarification. This enables us:

- to point out to someone inconsistencies in their behaviour
- to identify inconsistencies between what is said and what is done
- to clarify misunderstanding

* *Yesterday you said the statistics on the competitor products were an absolute priority. You are now saying that this proposal must*

227

be ready by tomorrow afternoon. As you can appreciate, both pieces of work will take some time and I am unclear of the priority. Which one do you want me to do first?

* *This morning when I asked if I could visit the London office you agreed wholeheartedly. I have just seen a circular to all members of staff in this office stating that no one in any circumstances can go to London. Could you please clarify the situation?*

* *You said in your appraisal that you wanted to be considered for promotion to a managerial position, yet you have refused to attend any of the management courses that all aspiring managers go through. What is your view about promotion?*

A calm and neutral voice ensures that there is no trace of blame or judgement about the inconsistency but instead a genuine attempt to resolve the confusion.

NOT BEING HEARD

When working through the assertion framework we may find that the other person is responding unreasonably and, we suspect, not listening to us. People do not listen for a number of reasons:

- they are heated and emotional
- they habitually behave aggressively or manipulatively

- they are choosing to ignore us
- they are intent on getting their own way
- they are preoccupied

When we feel we are not being listened to, a useful tip for re-establishing two-way communication is to address our concern in a non-aggressive manner.

* *I'm not sure that I'm making my point clearly. What do you think I am saying?*
* *Do you understand my view?*
* *What do you make of my position on this matter?*

This can focus attention on the process and reveal where no listening has happened so that we can convey our points. Most misunderstandings stem from inaccurate communication.

In extreme circumstances, a technique known traditionally as 'the broken record' helps us to:

- stand our ground
- refuse unreasonable requests
- say 'no'
- express an opinion or feeling when we do not feel heard

It should be used rarely and only when we feel that our position is threatened or our rights eroded.

To use the broken record we need to be clear about what we are saying and return to that particular sentence or phrase.

*   *'Thank you for offering, however I really don't
want a drink.'
'Go on – how can you have a good time without having a drink?'
'I'm enjoying the party enormously and I
really don't want a drink.'
'As the host it's my duty to make sure all my
guests have a good time. I don't want people
to think that I don't look after them.'
'I appreciate your concern, I am having a
good time and would prefer it if you would
stop pressing me to drink.'*

This technique will be perceived as aggression
unless we also respond by showing that we have
heard the other's view.

Michaela

*Michaela works as a manager in the information technology
division of a large retailing chain. There had been a few problems with a new system that had been developed. The information technology director had briefed all his managers that in no
circumstances were they to tell anyone the problems they were
having as he believed it was just a question of time before the
system was operational.*

*The finance director came into Michaela's office and asked
her what was happening with the system. She was in an awkward position. If she told the finance director, her boss would be
furious and would make her life difficult, and if she did not
disclose the information she would appear to be unhelpful. She
said to him, 'Tony, I'm not directly involved in the system. You
really will have to speak to Jack.'*

*Tony: 'Oh come on Michaela. you know what's going on. We
need to know and I can't get hold of Jack.'*

*Michaela: 'I'm sorry Tony, but I don't know the details, you
really will have to speak to Jack.'*

Michaela then stood up from behind her desk as if to leave.

Tony: 'Michaela you're being awkward, this is really important.'

Michaela: 'It's not my intention to be awkward. I have to go and sort something out. You really do need to speak to Jack.'

Tony walked out of the office.

EXPRESSING NEGATIVE FEELINGS

Telling someone how we feel by using the negative feelings approach is a way of expressing our feelings clearly yet professionally. Often the feelings get ignored but they will affect us and the relationship. Dealing with them in a non-aggressive way can help address the real issues.

The approach involves:

- describing the behaviour we are unhappy about
- explaining its effect on us, using 'I' statements
- stating what we would like to happen

For example:

* *For our last three one-to-one meetings you have allowed other members of staff to interrupt with routine queries and taken a number of telephone enquiries.*
* *I am unhappy about this as I do not have your full attention, which I value on serious detailed issues, and it is taking much more of my time than the half hour we always schedule.*
* *I would be grateful if we could be uninterrupted for the time that has been allocated, with*

231

the exception of emergencies, so that overall our one-to-one meeting will not take so long.

Ann

Ann was responsible for the marketing of several departments. She had been asked by the manager of one of her departments to show a new member of staff around whom she would be advising on a special conference he had been asked to organise. When she introduced him to her boss and explained the project they would be working on, her boss burst out laughing and said: 'You advise this poor chap on a conference of that scale. God help them!' Two other colleagues were present and also burst out laughing.

Ann felt really undermined in public and absolutely furious. She realised that it was not the right time to confront her boss. She waited a day until she had calmed down and asked for an appointment. Using the negative feelings approach and said to her boss. 'When I introduced Derek yesterday and told you about the special conference that I had been asked to advise on you burst out laughing and said "you – advise on this". I felt embarrassed as if my professional credibility was being questioned so publicly. This undermined not only me, but the standing of the department. I would prefer it if you are unhappy with my performance to confront me in private.'

OTHER PEOPLE'S ANGER

Many women feel frightened and intimidated when other people express their anger. In a fit of temper the person might make generalised undermining statements such as:

* *You are absolutely hopeless at your job. Look at what's happened now.*
* *Your organisation is so inefficient I'm taking my custom elsewhere.*

232

* *I'm furious at the way you dealt with that.*
* *You completely blew the contract.*

We disempower ourselves by completely backing down or by reacting with aggression. There are several practical things we can do to defuse the situation:

Allow the anger to be expressed

Ignoring the strength of feeling will in fact fuel it, so allowing the person to express their anger, provided we are in no physical danger, will be the most direct route to resolving the problem. If we suspect, however, that we may be in danger, the sensible course of action is to leave. Stopping any assumption we might make that we are automatically in the wrong and to blame for their feelings will help us to work through these stages.

Do not react with strong emotion

Reacting strongly will escalate the tension. Maintaining a calm level voice and open body language will be helped by not folding arms defensively, banging a hand on the table or shrinking into the seat. A conscious decision not to be intimidated will help us to project an assertive, open body posture.

Change the physical position or environment

This will help to defuse some of the tension in the situation, although care is needed when suggesting this to avoid sounding patronising. Getting both parties to the same physical level – preferably sitting – can neutralise any tension directed at us.

233

* *I can understand that you are angry and I would like to discuss the problem. However it will be easier if we do it in private.*

Demonstrate empathy

Acknowledging the anger of the person and repeating back their key points without admitting any fault will enable them to know we have listened and want to address the situation.

* *I can see why you would be annoyed regarding . . .*

* *Perhaps my organisation has been inefficient.*

Use active listening

We can get the full picture through listening intently and asking for more information with open questions to find areas of agreement or problem solving.

* *Can you tell me exactly what the problem is?*

Work towards a solution together

Once the person has discharged their anger and slowed down, suggesting that we can work together to find a mutually agreeable solution can help us to move on.

Anthea
Anthea is the fund-raising manager of a small charity. She has four members of staff reporting to her. One of the team, Emma, is most of the time very good at her job. From time to time,

however, she becomes awkward and unpredictable. On this occasion Anthea asked Emma to call back a sponsor who had expressed a specific interest in getting involved in their campaign.

Emma responded aggressively, 'They've already called back and they are not going to do anything.'

Anthea said calmly, 'Emma, I'd like you to call them back again and ask them specifically what they are prepared to do and find out what they had in mind when I had my original conversation with them.'

Emma retorted, 'I'm not doing it, you bloody do it.'

This scene was taking place in an open plan office in front of two other departments. Anthea felt humiliated, but decided to stand her ground and said 'Emma, I would like to talk to you at 3.30 in my office – will you be available?' to which Emma glared 'Ok'.

At 3.30 Emma sat with Anthea in her office. Anthea started by saying, 'Emma I''m really concerned about the display of anger that you expressed in front of everyone. Is there any reason why you were so hostile about making the phone call? I find it difficult to communicate with you when you shout at me like that.'

Emma replied, 'I had called the sponsor and they weren't very helpful. I felt as if you were showing me up in front of everyone. I thought as it was your contact you should deal with it. I felt angry about it.'

'I understand that you were unhappy about calling them and felt embarrassed. However, I am unhappy that you reacted in the way you did. Perhaps we can take the two issues separately?'

BULLYING

Bullying is an extreme and persistent expression of aggression, designed to intimidate and exert power over another person in a vindictive way. People who are bullied often feel that they are in some way responsible and this view is reinforced by the bullier as a way of denying responsibility.

Systematic bullying can be subtle and hard to pinpoint and over time it can be hard to maintain one's personal power in the onslaught. If we are bullied, it is essential to gain support from a colleague and raise the issue at work, following the guidelines outlined in the harassment section.

SEXUAL HARASSMENT

A recent Industrial Society survey, *No Offence?* (Stanford & Gardiner, 1993) , reported that 54% of women and 15% of men had at some stage of their working life experienced sexual harassment. The most common form was the language used by colleagues at work, with only a small minority having been physically abused.

Harassment can be very subtle but extremely invasive. It can have a devastating effect on the morale and performance of the victim. We believe that sexual harassment is:

Uninvited behaviour by a person against someone else that causes offence, embarrassment and tension in the workplace.

An important factor to bear in mind is that it is for the recipient to determine whether the behaviour is acceptable or not. It is the impact of the conduct on the victim, not the intent of the perpetrator, that is the determinant.

Examples of sexually harassing behaviour include:

- **Verbal**
  - *turning discussions to sexual topics*
  - *asking questions about personal or sexual life*
  - *telling sexual stories*
  - *making sexual innuendoes*
  - *sexual teasing, jokes, remarks*
  - *sexual comments about a person's clothing, anatomy or looks*
  - *patronising, derogatory remarks or references*
  - *repeated requests for dates or sexual favours*

- **Non-verbal**
  - *winking, leering, throwing kisses*
  - *making sexually suggestive gestures*
  - *displaying pornography or sexually suggestive materials*
  - *sexist graffiti*

- **Physical**
  - *unnecessary touching or patting*
  - *brushing against another's body*
  - *pinching*
  - *whistling*
  - *unwanted attention, letters, telephone calls*
  - *touching or rubbing oneself sexually in front of another*

237

- **The most serious incidents include:**

  - *actual or attempted rape or sexual assault*
  - *promises of job benefit in exchange for sexual favours*
  - *threat to job and/or prospects if sexual favours are not granted*

Women who complain of sexual harassment are often told that they are making a fuss about nothing, that they have no sense of humour, or that they are frigid or sexually naive. However, the type of behaviour that constitutes sexual harassment has nothing to do with a reciprocal romantic or flirtatious relationship. People who behave in this way are not trying to establish a personal relationship, but want to control and maintain power over someone else.

A very common form of sexual harassment in the workplace is the display or circulation of pornography or pin ups. A tribunal is unlikely to find a case for sexual harassment on the basis of pin-ups alone. This often forms part of an overall pattern. Although individuals' views on pin-ups and pornography differ, it must be accepted by management that it is inappropriate to display such materials in the workplace. Toleration of such materials by an employer gives a clear message of the organisation's attitude to women.

Statistics show that, despite many changes over the last fifteen years, women are still discriminated against at work. However, they are becoming far more aware of their rights and the type of support to which they are entitled, and the number of cases being brought to an industrial tribunal by women are increasing.

Tackling sexual harassment is not a route anyone takes without much thought. An important question we need to ask ourselves is: 'What are the consequences to me and to the organisation if I don't speak up?'

Shona

Shona works as a marketing assistant for a large computer company. She had been assigned to work with the marketing director, James, on the annual sales conference. Over a period of time James had made comments about her appearance and suggestive remarks about them getting together once the conference was over. At first Shona had just said 'thank you' to the compliments as she did not really want to acknowledge how uncomfortable she felt about the whole matter. It was when James started to make sexual innuendos about her appearance that she started to panic about the situation.

'I started to dread going into work and having sleepless nights. I told a couple of friends outside work and they said I should report him. What could I do? He is the marketing director after all. In the end I decided to speak to a senior woman manager, Kirstin, about the problem. She was very sympathetic and acknowledged I was in a difficult position. She advised me to write down everything he had said, including the date and the place, and to confront him with her. I thought I would die, but she assured me she would support me all the way. She suggested that if he didn't change his behaviour we would take it to the personnel director. I told her that I needed to think about it.

'Kirstin had a really good reputation for being kind and professional. I wrote down everything that had happened as she suggested and considered my options. If I let it carry on, it could get worse. If I did do something, there would be an atmosphere, but there was anyway, after the conference. Whatever I

239

decided, I knew I could not really win. So I took the risk and confronted him with her.

'I asked for a meeting with James and told his secretary it was a personal matter. Kirstin came along with me. He was rather surprised to see her as well and at first objected to her being there. I told him: "I've asked Kirstin to come specifically as I want her to witness and record what I am saying to you. I feel really distressed by your behaviour. On a number of occasions you have commented inappropriately about my appearance; for example, last Tuesday you said that you found my black suit was a real turn on. You have also made suggestive comments and implied that we should get together after the conference. I have made a record of all of these things. I would like you to stop making the comments and suggestions. If you continue to do this I will take it up with the personnel director."

He responded by saying: 'You are talking a load of nonsense. How on earth did you dream this lot up. If you don't want to work with me, then that can be arranged quite easily. I can get someone else who will jump at the opportunity. Don't threaten me sweetie, just because you've got a witness. What good is that going to do you?

Shona responded, shaking with fear: 'I would prefer it if I didn't have to work with you on this and I would like you to stop making the suggestive comments.'

James would not admit to Shona's accusations. She did stop working on the sales conference and told her boss it was due to a personality clash. She minimised contact with James and eventually asked for a transfer into the sales division.

What to do if you are being harassed

- Tell someone early on about what is going on for support.
- Make it clear to the harasser that their behaviour is unwelcome.
- Keep a written record of incidents as they

occur. Include date, place and time of incident and details of any witnesses.

- If there are no witnesses, report incidents to
  your colleague or union representative and
  ask them to take notes of what you are telling them.
- Check your organisation's policy on
  harassment.
- Raise the matter formally with someone who
  is in a position to take action, perhaps your
  line manager, personnel or a senior manager.
  Follow the grievance procedure if
  necessary.
- Find out if anyone else is being harassed by
  this person.
- If the organisation does not take you seriously and you have no union representation,
  seek external help from an organisation
  such as the Citizen's Advice Bureau. Write to
  your organisation informing them of your
  intention.

FRAMEWORK FOR DEALING WITH A HARASSER

- **State how you feel:**
  I feel angry that I have to speak to you about this.
  I am unhappy about your behaviour.
- **Describe the specific behaviour you do not like to the
  harasser:**
  *Every time you return a document to me, you touch my
  head and chest with your hands and arms.*
  *You comment on my legs and the length of my skirt when
  we are discussing business.*

241

- **State what you want to happen:**
  I do not want you to do that again.
  I would like you to stop immediately.
- **Say what you will do if the harassment continues:**
  If you continue to do this I will take the matter up with your manager and the personnel department.
- **Use the strategies for maintaining personal power**

Where to go for further advice:

Disciplinary procedure
Advisory, Conciliation and Arbitration Service (ACAS)
27 Wilton Street
London SW1X 7AZ
071–210 3000

Harassment
The Equal Opportunities Commission
Overseas House
Quay Street
Manchester M3 3HN
061–833 9244

The Commission for Racial Equality
Elliott House
10–12 Allington Street
London, SW1E 5EH
071–828 7022

The Industrial Society's Information Service
The Industrial Society
Robert Hyde House
48 Bryanston Square

London W1H 7LN
071–262 2401

The Institute of Personnel Management
IPM House
35 Camp Road
Wimbledon
London SW19 4UT
081–946 9100

WHEN THE GOING GETS TOUGH . . . IN LIFE

Maintaining personal power is an essential ability when the going gets really tough as a result of changes in our personal life.
For example:

- continuous implied criticism from a senior manager
- redundancy
- relationship breakdown
- disciplinary procedure against you
- serious family problem
- bullying

Our instinctive reactions to disaster or trauma can either help us to manage through the difficult time or make it worse. We might also have developed strategies for coping. Common reactions might include any of the following:

- ***Our health***
    - *neglecting our diet and eating more 'junk' food, drinking more coffee or alcohol, smoking more*
    - *taking greater care in our diet*

243

    – *curtailing or cancelling any regular activ-*
      ities that keep us in good health
      such as exercise class, swimming sessions,
      routine relaxation
    – *exercising more*

- ***The way we see it***
  – *taking it personally*
  – *reading more into the situation than is there*
    or jumping to conclusions
  – *catastrophising*
  – *rationalising*
  – *looking for the positive learning*
  – *reminding ourselves of the difficulties we*
    have overcome in the past
  – *trusting our capacity to cope*
  – *drawing support from our spiritual beliefs*
  – *getting in touch with our core values*
  – *boosting our self-esteem with positive*
    affirmation
  – *laughing*
  – *crying*

- ***Activity . . . or inactivity***
  – *rushing around in indiscriminate activity*
  – *writing endless lists*
  – *frantic cleaning*
  – *finding lots of tasks that we should have*
    done
  – *working quickly through tasks*
  – *taking to our bed*
  – *slowing right down in our movement and*
    activity
  – *cancelling engagements and commitments*
  – *staring into space*

- ***Support***
  - *sharing what is going on with friends or colleagues who we know will support us*
  - *running to trusted relatives or friends for comfort*
  - *blaming others and asking for sympathy*
  - *telling everybody how we feel*
  - *turning to our boss for support*
  - *using our professional association or network*

Looking back on times when it was necessary to maintain personal power, and using the list as a stimulus, it is useful to ask:

- What is my response pattern?
- Is it helpful?
- How can I modify any unhelpful actions so they support me more?
- Are there additional strategies I could draw upon?

We have responsibility for our reactions. Looking after ourself is one way of reclaiming some control, in addition to being a practical means of support. How we channel and renew our physical, mental and emotional energy will be significant in our capacity to cope.

Maintaining personal power is a way of protecting ourself from the knocks, preserving our strengths and mustering our resources. Sometimes it is about survival and coping as well as is possible. Essentially it relies on drawing strengths from previous success, making something positive out of an overload of negatives,

learning from the low spots and having com-
passion and tolerating our weakness and
vulnerability.

**FRAMEWORK FOR MAINTAINING PERSONAL
POWER**

- *Stop and think*
- *Maximise your stress strategies (see
  Chapter 3)*
- *Stick to your principles, beliefs and
  values, and ground yourself in them*
- *Consider the options*
- *Muster your supports*
- *Let some things go*
- *Assert your self-esteem with positive
  affirmation*

SUMMARY –
PRACTICAL TIPS

* Arrange regular one-to-one meetings with your staff and manager
* Be specific when giving criticism
* Encourage feedback on what you do well and the areas in which you could improve
* If distressed by negative feedback, ask for thinking time
* Smile and say 'thank you' when you receive a compliment
* Check out your organisation's disciplinary procedure
* Deal with difficult situations when they arise
* Practise saying 'no' when you feel overloaded
* Ask for clarification if you do not understand a situation
* Repeat your message if you feel you have not been heard
* Check out your organisation's policy on sexual harassment
* Think how you can positively support yourself through difficult times.

7

UNDERSTANDING ORGANISATIONAL POWER

The thing women have got to learn is that nobody gives you power. You just take it.

(Roseanne Barr)

POWER IN ORGANISATIONS

Effectiveness at work has much to do with power. If we want to progress in our organisation or get the best resources for our team and projects we must understand the nature of power within our organisation and acknowledge that power can be positive. This book has focused on empowering ourselves, but not at the expense of others. In organisations we can also use power in this way – and extend it to empowering others. It would be naive to expect that this is everyone's approach. However, we can learn by observing and use this knowledge to facilitate a use of power that squares with our values. In this chapter we:

- explore what power is and why it matters
- analyse politics and who is involved
- consider our own power and its potential
- examine who drives the organisation and the people who work there
- look at the factors for getting on and how to go about it

> * '*I didn't realise there were different types of power.'*
> * '*I used to think that power was something bad. I realise now the issue is not so much about what it is – it's about how you use it.'*
> * '*I used to cringe whenever the word power was mentioned, because it had such negative connotations for me.'*
> * '*I had never considered power in positive terms.'*
> * '*Once you have power, people's attitude towards you changes. In my organisation – they take you out to lunch.'*
> * '*To deny what you are and what you are capable of becoming is to deny your power – we've all got it, so why not enjoy it.'*

WHAT DO WE MEAN BY POWER?

Our definition of power is:

Power is the ability to get things done, and influence those around us, by mobilising internal and external resources in the pursuit of a goal.

We would suggest that power is a neutral concept – in itself it is neither good nor bad. It is how individuals choose to exercise it, inside or outside

249

the organisation, that influences our perception. This will determine our evaluation of power and the ease with which we embrace it.

* *'Despite the fact I hate the idea of politics, they do exist in my organisation.'*
* *'It's amazing to watch the behaviour of our senior management every time a new chief executive is appointed.'*
* *'I see politics as a neutral word. Whatever I do can be perceived as political depending on the agenda of the individual looking on.'*
* *'I have made a decision to be true to myself and my values.'*
* *'It just doesn't work to be upfront with some managers if you want to get along with them. I find I have to massage their egos first and we're not just talking about the men!'*
* *'I'm not comfortable with politics. I'm basically an open and honest person. I don't think in terms of being in the right place at the right time.'*
* *'I work on the basis that we'll do it their way first – because they are more senior or hold the budget; then if it doesn't work we can try mine. Call it politics, call it expediency – I have to live in the real world.'*
* *'I have learnt to listen more; it's important to understand where people are coming from.'*

CHARACTERISTICS OF PERSONAL POWER			
Powerless	Powerful	Empowers	Overpowers
Out of control	In control	Delegates/ shares control	Dominates
Uninformed	Informed	Informing	Witholds information
Helpless	Self-reliant	Helpful	Takes over or offers no help
Insecure	Confident and secure	Compliments Reinforces others' strengths	Arrogant
Inadequate	Capable	Trusts others' capabilities	Pushy Conceited
Fearful	Risk-taker	Offers others challenging opportunities and supports their efforts	Reckless Self-absorbed

WHY POWER MATTERS IN ORGANISATIONS

If individuals are to gain and exercise power
effectively it is important to understand why it is
so valued by men and women in the workplace.
Whether or not power is used wisely will depend
on the perspective of the individual.

- **Power provides us with greater choice**
  If we do not like what is going on in our organisation with power we are more able to exercise choice or make changes. The alternatives are to accept and tolerate the situation or to leave.
- **Individuals with power are taken more seriously**
  Powerful people are listened to about the way the organisation is run. They can make decisions that have an impact on others, including, for example, influencing who else gets promoted.
- **Powerful people have greater access to the best resources**
  Getting access to the best possible people and resources helps us achieve the outcomes that ultimately benefit the organisation as a whole. In the process we can also benefit ourself, our manager, our team and colleagues.
- **Progression is determined by powerful people**
  Our overall career progress in the organisation will by influenced by our performance, which in turn depends on being able to get things done and on the opinion of those who are in power. Power grows power, yet it is not just about our position in the organisation.

ORGANISATIONAL POLITICS

In organisations, 'politics' describes the activities that concern the acquisition of power and the competition for it between various interest groups as they attempt to influence events, decisions and outcomes to suit their particular objectives.

Many women on our courses view organisational politics with revulsion and do not want to participate. They associate politics with manipulation or playing unfairly, or simply resent the time they see as wasted in its pursuit, time that could be spent doing the job. Often an assumption is made that politics is only for personal ends. By missing the connection between effectiveness and influence, and failing to appreciate the political aspect of workplace relationships, we deny ourselves opportunities for power.

Political decisions can encompass making a thousand people redundant, issuing all members of staff with childcare vouchers, leaving a subordinate's name off a crucial document to which they contributed or telling our manager about the excellent work carried out by another colleague. If we want to make a difference, power and politics are essential.

PEOPLE AND POLITICS

Baddeley and James (1987) describe four approaches to politics in organisations:

- **'Wise owls'** are genuinely concerned for the overall interests of the organisation and recognise that everyone is vying for influence and resources for their own or the organisation's agenda. They understand the need to be politically aware in order to take the organisation forward. They have a strong sense of values, think before they speak, act assertively, share information, and give and get support.

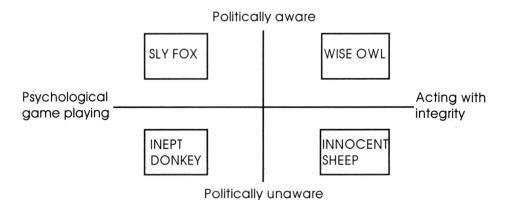

- **'Innocent sheep'** want the organisation to succeed but do not want to get involved with politics. By adopting this stance they are handing their power to the active players and consequently become subject to their decisions. They tend to rely on authority and expertise, stick to the professional rules, have a great sense of loyalty and believe you must be right if you are powerful.
- **'Sly foxes'** are politically aware, but use the organisation to fulfil their personal goals, regardless of those of the organisation. Thinking before speaking, they have a charming veneer and do not display feelings openly. They tend to make the rules work to suit them and get support through manipulation on a win/lose basis.
- **'Inept donkeys'** are not aware of the political dynamics and the different competing interests. They are obvious about striving to achieve their personal goals at the expense of the organisation, yet are oblivious to the impact of their own and others' behaviour.

As with other behavioural styles, we will all play all of these roles according to the circumstances and need to be aware of our behaviour, its implications and outcomes. Do we, like an innocent sheep, hand over our power to others and become a pawn in their game, or do we want to stumble on unsuccessfully like an inept donkey? If the latter, are we solely concerned with our own interests? Do we use the different agendas and competing interests of our colleagues to further our personal aims, regardless of the impact on the organisation, like a sly fox, or do we recognise that, by working with different groups, we can take the organisation forward and empower others in the process, like the wise owl? The choice is ours.

WHAT GIVES US POWER?

Power is not just about our position. People in organisations will have different types of power. Formal power is vested in the individual by their position, is usually gained by promotion through a formal route and is often the gift of more senior managers. It is usually accompanied by the type of power that is acquired more informally, which does not depend on the person's status in the hierarchy. An important influence on our informal power is how we and other people see it.

FORMAL POWER

Formal power goes with the job title and the remit of authority and is generally accepted by others. It often carries some capacity to reward, to allocate or control resources or to remove obstacles.

* *A sales director of a computer company helps a manager do their job more effectively by providing them with an upgraded car, enhanced technology, or an extra person.*

* *The production director of a large manufacturing company decides that redundancies will not be based on a 'last in, first out' policy, as specified in the company handbook, but chooses to use the redundancies as an opportunity to get rid of the people perceived as 'dead wood'.*

* *The staff see their role as implementing the departmental manager's plan for generating business, which they do not question unless invited to do so.*

INFORMAL POWER

Informal power can come from the following:

* **Interpersonal power** – others respond to us because of our interpersonal skills and the appeal of our personality.

  * *Cassie is highly regarded by important clients and has an assertive confidence. She is able to say things to senior managers that others at her level would not dare because they lack the charismatic clout to carry it off.*

- **Expertise** – others perceive us as having some special knowledge or skills that are essential to the organisation.

  * *The information technology manager in an organisation has, with external consultants, designed the systems for the company and has cultivated an illusion that they are complex. This has put her in a powerful position as she is the only one perceived to understand the system, and is highly valued for her skills and knowledge by the other senior managers.*

- **Resource control** – our power is based on having access to important resources or information, including staff, equipment, finances or time, which help others accomplish their goals. People who hold this type of power do not necessarily also have formal power, for example:
  - caretakers with responsibility for space and equipment
  - secretaries who hold the diaries of powerful people
  - anyone who holds a cross-functional budget or has accountability for people

---

EXERCISE – YOUR POWER BASE

- Using the headings above, identify your present power base.
- See how you could extend it.

Roberta

Roberta worked as a tax specialist for a large multinational corporation. Her office was next to the car park, so that when she came in to work she saw very few people. Because she was employed for her expertise, the only people who knew about her were other accountants and some staff who needed her knowledge. She would normally work through lunch at her desk.

She had been doing the job for three years and was conscious of the fact that many of her contemporaries had been promoted or moved on to gain broader experience. She talked to an old friend one weekend about her frustration. Her friend said to her: 'Why does the company employ you?' She replied: 'Because I'm really good at my job.' Her friend said: 'It's not enough to be good at your job, you need to be known by people and have a wide range of skills to be an effective manager – your specialism isn't enough.'

Roberta thought hard about the comments her friend had made and decided on a plan of action. She stopped parking the car next to her office and moved it to the other side of the building, so that when she walked through the maze of corridors she would say good morning to everyone she passed.

She made a point of having lunch in the staff restaurant and plucked up the courage to talk everyone, regardless of their status. Through chatting to people over lunch she started to learn about the the different working parties in the company and in time asked to join. By joining she found she developed new skills, found out more about the organisation and the training opportunities it provided, and also developed a powerful network of contacts.

Roberta is now one of the most powerful senior managers in her organisation. Her power base has extended beyond expertise to include formal, resource control and interpersonal power.

GENERATING POWER

Knowing what drives the organisation and the people in it can help us to develop power and gives us a framework for channelling our energy and achieving acceptance and success.

WHO DRIVES THE ORGANISATION?

Groups of people with vested interests, both outside and within every organisation, will determine its direction, issues and agenda.

The big picture

In order to succeed in our workplace world we have to think beyond our immediate jobs and see the big picture. External stakeholders – which can include the shareholders, competitors, the government, clients, suppliers, customers and the customer chain, depending on the type of business or environment in which you operate – shape the political, economic, social and technological position of the business. Their agendas can change the whole focus of an organisation.

The senior people interviewed by Forrest and Tolfree (1992) spoke about the importance of developing external connections that would carry the organisation forward. They stated that at their level they left the day-to-day running of the organisation to their managers; their role was to provide vision within the wider context. The more senior we become in our work, the more essential this ability will be. In the 1980s, Thatcherism set a trend of commercialising institutions such as the NHS, government departments and local authorities. This has brought change in the way business is conducted, which has demanded new skills and work practices. A more competitive approach, whether in the private, public or voluntary sectors, constantly seeks new ways of managing, monitoring and enhancing the service. Understanding our organisation as a dynamic force that is constantly undergoing and creating change will provide us with insights for its future success and the opportunities that change will bring. It also helps us to target our activities more relevantly.

Bernadette

Bernadette worked as a manager in a large hospital. She was studying for a management diploma and had decided that her project would focus on the reduction of patients' waiting times for her department's clinics, in line with the Patient's Charter. She involved staff at every level of the organisation, from the consultants through to the administrative staff. She enlisted the help of the quality manager to research patients' problems with the current system and to find out the level of service they expected.

As a result of her work the organisation of the patients' clinics was changed to ensure a minimal waiting period. She has been given recognition for her work and has given presentations to various colleagues and a group of MPs. Several managers and consultants from other hospitals have visited her to find out how she devised their current system.

Lysette

Lysette works as a manager in the voluntary sector. She recognised that, in order for her organisation to benefit from the system of contracting out of services by local authorities, the emphasis of her department would have to change considerably. It would mean the organisation would have to become competitive in providing a quality service for their new client group – the local authorities. She put a proposal to her chief executive. As a consequence of her initiative she has become a director.

260

EXERCISE –
THE BIG PICTURE

- To help you focus on where your organisation fits in a wider frame, ask yourself the following questions:

  How well do you understand the nature of your business?

  If your organisation is a small part of a much larger operation, how does it fit in?

  Who are your external stakeholders?

  What is the current thinking about the future of your business?

  To which external groups does your organisation need to promote itself positively?

  Do you understand the chain of events that takes place to deliver your end product or service?

  Who could you approach for sources of information and insights?

- Gain relevant information. This will demand creativity and access to specific sources:

  Could you attend the annual general meeting or its equivalent?

  Do you know and read all the trade journals for your industry?

  Do you make a point of reading a quality newspaper each day?

  Does the local newspaper give information about your industry, your clients and your suppliers?

  Have you ever taken the opportunity to attend relevant conferences?

  Who could advise you on information sources?

  What career opportunities are there?

Lorraine

Lorraine had recently been promoted to a new sales position. She had been doing the job successfully for about six months when the managing director asked her to attend an exhibition in Germany. He told her that it was not very important, but he wanted her to go and see what their competitors were doing.

'We didn't even have an exhibition stand. All I had brought with me was a bag of samples and leaflets, as I had been told not to make much of an effort. I saw this as an opportunity for me to get to know our suppliers and competitors. One of our suppliers actually let me use his stand to promote our samples. It was really useful talking to our competitors, because it turned out we weren't competing on exactly the same products and services. We exchanged customer information on possible development opportunities for our businesses. My managing director was really impressed with the information I had gathered from an exhibition that wasn't really that important.'

The key players

The internal stakeholders are the people within the organisation who have a say in what results are achieved and how they are achieved. Working within the management structure, they create the culture of the organisation, which determines who has power, how it is used and what we have to do to get on. These key players generate the issues for the organisation. At times of rapid change the alliances within this group will become more significant, may shift and have more impact on our area. In addition, the backgrounds of the key players, and whether their profile is changing, will be an interesting indicator for the future direction.

Lauren

Lauren works as the public relations executive for a firm of accountants. The managing partner for the firm had decided to launch a quality care for client programme and invited all apparently relevant departments to send a representative along to the planning meeting.

'I wasn't actually invited, but I had a background in research and I could see the link the between my function and the objectives of the programme. When I approached the training manager he was delighted for me to get involved. I believe the firm benefited from my skills and I certainly received an enormous amount from the experience. Apart from raising my profile with the managing partner, I was invited to help deliver the training. It meant I met 300 people out of our 700 staff and overcame my fear of public speaking. As I work in a fee-earning environment, I suspect many people actually wonder what I do – this activity gave them some insight into the nature of some of my work.'

If we wish to progress and gain power we must be perceived as being appropriate for the organisation and acting in appropriate ways. This demands an eye on the future as well as an awareness of the past and present. It also forces us to confront our own values. Working effectively in an organisation is impossible if we are pretending to be something we are not. Sometimes this can force us to make choices about where and how we progress our careers.

Hazel

Hazel's position was being made redundant as a result of a massive downsizing programme. 'I had been assured that I could be redeployed, but the job they were offering me did not inspire me at all. A senior woman had been asked to develop our customer service function – it sounded new and really exciting. I researched all the skills that would be required to work in

263

> ## EXERCISE –
> ## THE KEY PLAYERS
>
> • Ask yourself:
>
> Who are the key players – past and present – in my organisation?
> What are the current issues in which they are involved?
> How are the current trends different from past trends?
> What do I think will be the issues of the future?
> How do the key players relate to each other? In what ways are they similar or different?
> Who is allied to whom and why? Are they all from similar backgrounds and roles or is the profile changing, and how?

this new area and carried out a skills inventory on myself. I found I had to include a lot of experience that had been gained outside of work. I wrote a letter to the woman expressing my interest in what she was doing and highlighting to her the experience that could be of value to her. She called me for an interview and I got a really great job.'

HOW DO WE MAKE PROGRESS?

To understand the required profile for succeeding we need to examine the people who hold the significant power bases of our organisation and also find out how we are perceived by the key players.

Research by the Equal Opportunities Commission has shown that, although women are succeeding in gaining professional and work-related qualifications, their lack of broad management experience is preventing them from breaking into senior management. In industry and the service sectors we tend to get caught up with the expertise power base in the 'pink ghettos' or 'velvet grottos' of personnel, education, administration, training and marketing rather than gaining experience in the 'traditionally male route to promotion', which provides the formal authority power bases.

Research into what influences promotion has identified three distinct factors (reported in Willis & Daisley 1990):

- **Performance** – 10%
  By itself this is not enough, yet it underpins everything we do.

- **Image** – 30%
  This is about whether the type of person we are and how we come across is acceptable in our particular organisation.

- **Visibility** – 60%
  Performance and image have no value unless the key people know about us and our achievements.

Many women accept that these statistics make a lot of sense of what is happening in organisations, yet feel uncomfortable with them. Clearly all three factors are interrelated.

265

```
┌─────────────────────────────────────────┐
│                                         │
│              EXERCISE –                 │
│            WHO GETS ON?                 │
│                                         │
│  •  Answer the following questions:     │
│                                         │
│     Who are the people who epitomise your│
│     organisation?                       │
│     What characterises them?            │
│     What are their qualifications?      │
│     What do people have to do to get on │
│     where you work?                     │
│     Is there a classic route to senior  │
│     management?                         │
│                                         │
└─────────────────────────────────────────┘
```

PERFORMANCE

Our performance is not something to take lightly, even though it accounts for only a small part of our promotability.

If we want to progress within our organisation then we need to be thinking strategically about the skills that will help us to move forward. We generally get promoted on what we can bring to the position rather than on what we need to learn so seeking out opportunities and asking for training in these areas is essential preparation.

Adding value

In general, people get promoted not because they have done a good job in terms of the confines of their job description but because of activity that demonstrates commitment and initiative beyond the boundaries of the job.

The people who are highly rated are the ones

266

who add value. This could be through turning a failure into a success, demonstrating enterprise, identifying a new market, or developing a new product. Capitalising on being first in a new position, bringing about effective organisational change or taking a major risk and succeeding are the hallmarks of the extraordinary in most organisations.

If we want to move on in our organisation we must show that we can move the organisation on. This involves shifting the focus of what we do to tasks that take an organisation, department or team forward and that have strategic value.

Martina

Martina had been assigned to work on a project that involved the development of a computerised customer administration system for the company's many branches. The initial projection was that it would take over three years to get people trained up on it. She realised the company did not have the time and decided to talk to the women who would have to administer it about how they could learn the system. Through her discussions with them they came up with the idea of developing a training disk, a manual and a helpline. The staff could be up and running on the system with just two days' intensive training by themselves.

The discussions with the administrators had revealed to Martina that all the branches had different definitions of the term 'valuable customer'. She asked a random sample of the branches to provide her with the data on 600 valuable customers. Charting the information revealed a fundamental lack of consistency in the customer profile and therefore an enormous loss of potential income for the company.

She decided to approach one of the board directors with her information. He asked her to give a presentation to the board. As a result of her work she was asked significantly promoted.

267

> ### EXERCISE –
> ### ADDING VALUE
>
> - Explore the areas that you can see need developing that go beyond the job description and provide opportunities to add value.
>
> - Choose one and plan how you will work towards its completion without neglecting your other work.

Maintaining that we are too busy with the current role to do anything extra or that we will tackle the project when times are quieter (which of course they never are) will keep us in the same position. Making time to progress on an added value project will help us make our mark.

Finger on the pulse

Women often get ghettoised in non-relevant areas, focusing all their attention on doing their job and not looking beyond it, or become the expert on something peripheral to the main thrust of the business. Nor do we always see the significance of knowledge to our performance in the job.

To be relevant in the organisation we must know its primary purpose. The more we are attuned to current issues and recurring themes and alert to emerging trends, the more able we are to focus our work effectively. Aligning ourself and our team with the direction of the business provides opportunities for synergistic development of the organisation and our career.

Henrietta
Henrietta works as an office manager for a specialist design consultancy. 'My job was to manage the office staff and customer enquiries. One day an enquiry came in from Belgium. We have a sales team who cover most countries interested in our particular field, but no one has ever developed business in Belgium, so there was no obvious person to prepare the quotation. I decided to prepare the quotation. I waited until the next day when a director came in and showed him my work. He said I could send it from me.

'The work from Belgium materialised and as no one seemed to take an interest in it I took responsibility for it. As a lot of business has been generated out of this client I now visit them regularly and have developed my skills as a sales consultant.'

To get information we need to tap into the informal networks, build relationships with key people, observe how resources are allocated for certain projects, monitor competitors and use all the additional sources of information already referred to in this chapter.

Siobhan
Siobhan is a headteacher. 'I never saw myself as just a teacher or restricted by the grade I was paid. I made a point of attending meetings, not only to find out what was going on, but also to see what needed doing.'

> ## EXERCISE –
> ## RELEVANCE
>
> - Describe the primary purpose of the organisation.
>
> - What are the short- and long-term objectives of the organisation? If you are not sure, start to find out.
>
> - How close are your activities to the primary purpose?
>
> - Could they be closer?

Lee

Lee works in publishing. 'There are always things that people won't do that you can make your own, in order to make your mark. My first mistake was becoming known as the grammar expert – terribly useful for everyone else but not for my development. I am now the person who knows about new business.'

Beulah

Beulah is a senior civil servant. 'There are not many promotion opportunities at the moment. However, I am well aware that the activities in which I have become involved are all to my benefit in the future. Apart from the fact that involvement in extra areas of the job makes my work more interesting, I see them as my training ground for my next position. In addition I am becoming better known to the senior management team.'

Capitalising on our appraisal

Our appraisal or performance review is an ideal opportunity to take stock of how we are doing in our job and to let our manager know of our achievements and aspirations. We might expect our

270

> *   '*I was annoyed that I had not been considered for internal promotions and raised it with my manager. He said, "I thought you were happy where you are, you do such a good job." I hadn't discussed my career aspirations with him at all.*'
> *   '*My boss ignored the areas I had really worked hard in and picked out my most obvious achievements in my appraisal as that's what she knew. I realised that I had to help her next time, so I wrote a list of all the things I had been working on. I did this too when I applied for a new post to help my manager's reference writing.*'

manager to know about all of our achievements – and indeed they might. However, they will not know the detail of our skills, so two-way communication is essential. Similarly they will not know what we want from our careers unless we tell them. It can be useful to remember that the manager might find appraisal uncomfortable and we can help the process by:

– agreeing an agenda beforehand
– at the end of the appraisal agreeing short-term and long-term objectives, with measure-able criteria

At a time when organisations are coping with fewer managers and more flexible teamworking and often expecting longer hours, it is harder for managers to know exactly what every member

---

EXERCISE –
PREPARING FOR APPRAISAL

- To aid your preparation ask yourself the following questions:

  What are the problems I have solved?
  How have I increased revenue?
  How have I saved money?
  Where have I taken on additional responsibility?
  What are my greatest achievements?
  How can I demonstrate my relevance?
  What do I want to do next?
  What extra areas can I take on to show spare capacity?

---

of their team is doing. We can make it easier for them by keeping a record of the things we have done well throughout the year and highlighting our achievements at our one-to-one meetings. It is worth actually checking with our manager how they will be measuring our performance.

Many women feel more comfortable talking themselves down than saying what they have done well. A useful approach is to make a concentrated effort to talk ourself up and leave the areas that need to be improved to our manager to bring up. It is also worth using this time to ask for any help we need in achieving our objectives.

Constant learning

The world we live in is constantly undergoing change and requiring more of us. If we want to get on – or even remain in employment – it is our responsibility to ensure that we receive adequate training that updates our skills and knowledge.

Research has shown that women tend to receive less management and professional training than their male counterparts. We do not always ask and it is easy to put the pressures of our day-to-day work above our own development. However, there will be long-term benefits from attending as many relevant courses as possible. The benefits are to do not only with refining and enhancing our skills and knowledge base, but with acquiring useful contacts on in-house and public courses.

IMAGE – DOES YOUR FACE FIT?

If we want to move into a more senior position we need to think how our personal image and communication style will fit the next level. Senior managers are appointed because of their understanding of the big picture and their ability to handle higher-level meetings, teams and clients, and because of others' confidence in them to deliver.

The way we behave in routine and extraordinary situations will send out messages about our future potential including:

- our technical and interpersonal skills and abilities
- our confidence
- our capacity to represent the organisation
- our toughness

273

> *   'Attending in-house and external courses really keeps me on my toes. I always attend courses with an open mind, because, apart from picking up skills and tips, I have made some really useful contacts within the organisation and outside. The key is to stay in touch.'
>
> *   'I have always been fascinated by how organisations work. I know in our particular sector we are constantly going through change. Reading about management theory and practice and the latest developments in the business helps me to keep up-to-date and has helped me see different ways of tackling problems – which has enabled me to build my credibility with other managers and increased my self-confidence.

EXERCISE –
MANAGE YOUR OWN LEARNING

- Identify the skills and knowledge that will help your career and development.

- Explore the opportunities for acquiring them.

- Draft a plan to ensure you are regularly updating and learning.

Looking the part for the next promotion

Whether we like it or not, our dress and behaviour send out powerful signals about our confidence and authority. Our image has to fit with the culture, although we may not want to completely align ourself with the past or the present and instead want to make additional statements through our image. Looking at the dress of women at least two levels above us in our organisation will give us some pointers – which we may or may not adopt. If there are no women above, it is worth looking at senior women who work for competitors, or at professionals in the same field.

In general, it is worth selecting clothes that do not attract too much attention to our appearance, so that people focus on what we say and do rather than on what we look like. Clothes also must be sufficiently comfortable and practical so we can forget what we look like and focus on the job. The most important factor is to decide how we want to present ourselves – and this will be very personal.

Rebecca

'I remember vividly a senior woman speaking on the Pepperell Management Development Course asking two women to stand up – one was wearing a cardigan and the other one was wearing a suit. She asked us which one was the manager. Although we didn't like to comment, we all agreed that it was the woman wearing the suit.'

Danielle

'As a senior woman manager I find the spotlight is on me. This can have real advantages, which I play to. I believe in dressing

275

professionally for all meetings. However I do not want to dress like a man or become another black/grey/black suit – so when it is appropriate I wear vivid green, red or pink. I know I cannot be ignored and it really helps when I want to speak up at a meeting.'

Speaking the part for the next promotion

In Chapters 5 and 6 we covered some specific ways of tackling difficult situations. Speaking with confidence about our ideas, ourselves and our opinions is essential if people are going to take us seriously.

* *A senior manager commented that it was noticeable with some women who were being interviewed that when they spoke about achievement they would talk in terms of what 'we had achieved', giving credit to their team and minimising their own part in it. All of the men spoke in terms of what 'I have achieved and how I have made a difference'. The women seemed uncomfortable acknowledging their achievement. She believes that there needs to be a balance between the two approaches.*

If we have problems blowing our own trumpet, it is possible to let people know what we have achieved naturally. When someone asks after us, we can respond positively by relating our experiences through interesting anecdotes or by telling colleagues what we have been doing.

* *I'm feeling really good today because my client has just signed a big contract.*

* *I'm having a really good day because I've just seen the press results on my product launch and they are the highest we've ever attained.*
* *I met a very interesting contact when I gave a speech at the conference I attended on behalf of the organisation.*

Coping with stress for the next promotion

How we cope under pressure will be an important indicator to the decision-makers. If we can project a positive and realistic attitude, especially when the going gets tough, the more seriously we are going to be taken when the promotion opportunity arises. In addition, how we cope with failure and learn from it will reveal our level of maturity and resilience.

As we discussed in Chapter 3, work–life balance is essential if we are to be effective in our jobs and we may need to boost our stress strategies to support us through periods of change or increased responsibility. If we are having a tough time at home or at work it is advisable to guard against extreme displays of emotion, as people will resent dealing with our behaviour rather than the particular issue; we need to build in ways to release emotion elsewhere.

The more we take on, the more important effective time management becomes. Thinking ahead, always being punctual and building in additional time for checking projects and reports so that they are delivered on time or earlier than the deadline all convey our capacity to progress.

VISIBILITY

Sending out the smoke signals

If our performance is to enhance our power it must be known to other people. It is difficult to become known if we work in a very large organisation. Examples of some ways of getting noticed:

- join working parties or special project groups
- speak up at public meetings
- go to leaving parties attended by senior management
- eat in the staff restaurant
- send copies of praise from the clients to the manager and anyone else who has a stake in promoting a positive image of your organisation
- apply for internal promotion before you are ready in order to get an idea of the qualities and strengths that senior managment are looking for so you can start acquiring them
- join the company's golf team
- put your name on ideas, notes of meetings and documents you have produced

Visibility and image must be supported by substance. The opportunities to show our achievements and those of our team or department must be appropriate to our organisation and its culture.

Petra
'I had a long-term goal of wanting to go into senior manage-ment. I thought, as I'm going to be working most of my adult life

and I want to make a difference, why not go for it? I didn't get on with my boss and I didn't know what was really required, so for the hell of it I applied for different positions as they came up. This has had three benefits. Firstly it enabled me to find out what they are looking for and to start preparing for a serious go at it. Secondly, because I knew I wasn't really ready for the promotion I was actually quite relaxed, and thirdly it brought to their attention that I was interested in moving up. Since having had a few dummy runs, I have now been promoted into a position I really wanted.'

Lavinia
'I've been working as editor of our company newsletter for two years. It's only recently that I've started to put my name on it as I didn't think anyone would be interested, but they do need to know what I do.'

Trudy
'I entered my team for the company quiz and we won. This was absolutely wonderful for their profile as people in the company now know who to approach for our expertise. I was asked to give a talk on a difficult piece of legislation that related to our industry at the last annual general meeting.'

Marilyn
'My company was setting up more and more outlets throughout the world but the chances for me ever going on company business seemed to be diminishing day by day. I decided to pay for myself to go on a working trip on the understanding that it would not be taken away from my holiday entitlement. I worked extremely hard and produced some excellent results. The managing director recognised what I had done and agreed to reimburse my flight and hotel accommodation. The next time the opportunity arose it was all paid for. In my industry you have to prove yourself all the way, not only to be as good as the men, but better than them.'

EXERCISE –
VISIBILITY

- Ask yourself:

  Who knows or could be told about my career aspirations?
  Where and how could I communicate my career aspirations? For example:
  – appraisal
  – one-to-one meetings
  – organisational gatherings
  – lunch with colleagues
  What are the working parties or project groups I could join?
  What organisational social activities could I join?

Sara

Sara works as a personnel officer in the pharmaceutical industry. 'On two separate occasions, over an 18-month period, our human resources officers had been on maternity leave. In both instances I really wanted to have a go at doing their jobs, but I didn't have the confidence to ask. When the opportunity arose again in my appraisal I told my boss what I would like to do. He was really surprised as he didn't think I was interested. He said I could certainly have a go and I needn't wait until my appraisal.'

Handling meetings

We convey our credibility wherever we have the attention of others. Much of our contact with them will take place at formal meetings, so how we handle the situation is critical in terms of our image.

280

> * 'I was terrified when I went to my first management meetings, but I learnt to speak up within the first ten minutes. They don't remember everything you've said anyway.'
> * 'I find it useful to observe the behaviour of people around the table – you can learn a lot from them.'
> * 'The key for me is to focus on the purpose of the meeting and to forget myself. I think in terms of what can I bring to this to make it worth while for myself and my colleagues. If I can't do anything, it's worth just listening and learning from what is going on.'

Many women report anxiety about meetings and problems with speaking up, being heard and being given credit for their ideas. A common response can be to behave passively, but if we never speak up other people will never form an opinion of us. For many of us it means taking a risk and voicing our opinion and experience. How many of us have felt really frustrated when we have been bursting with an idea and then someone else says it and gets the credit?

We have to accept the fact that everyone – including the men – will be nervous at a new meeting. However, there are some practical things we can do to help ourselves.

281

POINTERS FOR MEETINGS

- Prepare beforehand – read the minutes and agenda and check your understanding with someone else. If you cannot get a copy of the agenda until the meeting, introduce yourself to the chair and ask for clarification of any points of unfamiliarity.

- Listen to the discussion and not to any negative inner dialogue.

- Decide where to sit so that you are not excluded from the discussion, caught up between totally opposing perspectives or denied the chairperson's attention.

- Maintain assertive body language.

- If nervous, speak early – either to ask a question or to agree with someone. 'The mouse at the meeting rule' is about ensuring people know you are there within the first ten minutes. If you do not speak up it just gets harder.

- If you want to make an important point and your brain is racing, quickly jot down the key words, take a deep breath and speak very slowly, quietly and deliberately.

- If someone interrupts you, use the person's name – a useful technique to get their attention – by saying: 'Peter, I hadn't quite finished. As I was saying . . .' and look the person in the eye.

- If there is someone you trust at the meeting, ask them for feedback on your performance. They will be flattered to be asked their opinion and to have their experience valued.

Dorothy

'A more senior colleague took the credit for something I had worked really hard at. He actually told the managing director in front of everyone that he had pulled off a deal with which he had very little to do. I was furious and realised that being a nice girl was not going to get me anywhere with this chap. I had been taught not to upset others, but I realised that this would always happen if I didn't stand my ground. This particular man was also a real bully and highly manipulative. I weighed up I would have more to lose if I didn't deal with it.

'I arranged a meeting with my head of department and this man. The head of department was uncomfortable about the whole thing. I knew I would not get either of them to admit in public that I had done all the work – all I actually wanted was the guy to own up to me that what he did was wrong. At first he patronised me about being a little woman. I just said, 'Would you agree that taking the credit for the work you didn't do was totally unfair?' He then got aggressive with me. I kept repeating the sentence. He made comments about my size and I kept repeating the sentence. It was really tempting to get upset and fly off the handle, but I would have just played into his hands. Finally he had to agree.

'I was never given the credit for that bit of work, but the word went out that I was not a woman you messed around with and he certainly never crossed my path again. It was the first time I accepted that for my own self-esteem and professional credibility I would have to learn to stand my ground – it certainly had a ripple effect!'

> ## SUMMARY –
> ## PRACTICAL TIPS
>
> *   Identify your power bases
> *   Read a quality national newspaper and trade journals to understand the big picture for your organisation
> *   Identify the skills you will need for your next job
> *   Identify a task that will add value for your organisation and tell someone senior what you are doing
> *   Prepare all your positive points for your appraisal
> *   Select the courses you need to do your job effectively and prepare your case for your manager
> *   Dress for success
> *   Tell people the difference you and your team make to the organisation
> *   Join a project group or working party that will take your organisation forward
> *   Apply for promotion for the experience and to send out the signals

8

BUILDING POWERFUL RELATIONSHIPS

'I have learnt that I don't have to behave like a man to operate in a man's world. I can work effectively as a woman in a world made for both men and women.'
(Christine Garner)

WHY RELATIONSHIPS IN WORK MATTER

The nature and quality of our relationships with people connected with our work – either inside or outside the organisation – will affect our effectiveness, enjoyment and success in the workplace.

Most of us rely on other people to achieve our objectives and implement plans in our organisations. Others, of course, may also be dependent on us. Good-quality relationships can enhance our personal power in the work-place and put us in a stronger position to empower those around us. As organisations are taking away tiers of management, leaving flatter structures, greater emphasis on team-based working is demanded. This style requires high-quality relationships, not just within the team but across the organisation. Getting things done is helped by using the contacts we already have and developing those that will assist our work in the future. By recognising the reciprocal nature of our relationships at

285

work we can identify ways of enhancing them further.

Broader and more productive relationships also get us, our team and what we bring to an organisation known, while the insights gained through such relationships help us appreciate the breadth of the business, giving us greater choices for future involvement. As discussed in Chapter 7, visibility is also significant to promotion. In other words, who actually knows about us, within and beyond the organisation, will affect our career prospects. For instance, Research by InterExec (1993) has revealed that 70% of male executives get new jobs as a result of whom they know.

This chapter explores the benefits and the means of developing significant relationships with our external networks, and with our manager, peers, team, sponsors and mentors.

NETWORKING

Networking can sound more complex or pompous than it is. At its most basic it is about talking to people. We define it as **the process of building relationships of mutual benefit to both parties**. This can involve:

- exchanging information
- making introductions
- offering encouragement, advice or support
- providing practical help

As with all that we have covered in this book, networking is about not only what we do but also how we do it: action and the attitudes that drive it. To be satisfactory and satisfying for all parties involved, networking should be based on mutual respect and trust – and be fun.

Women often network naturally. Because of the nature of our roles, many of us willingly help other people and rely on other people's help to manage all the elements of our lives. Women's informal friendship groups and more formal circles for community activities, family support, childcare and enjoyment are based on networking. In these groups we start by building rapport on which we can base a relationship of trust. We would not let just anyone pick up our children from school or house-sit to feed the cats when we are away. In addition, we look for some degree of reciprocity. It is not that we expect something back for all that we do, but that the relationship suffers if it is completely one-sided. Good networks develop over time and are fuelled by communication.

The same principles apply when we network in the workplace arena and as it is a way of creating and maintaining relationships it is an important activity. Managing the networking in ways that we feel comfortable with can help us to enjoy the process of talking, finding out about people and building relationships. Before we can achieve that we need to be clear about the factors that get in the way of us having a go at it.

BARRIERS TO NETWORKING

There are a whole host of reasons why women choose to reject networking. The word can have strong connotations of the 'old boys' network: from which we are generally excluded. In the report *The Key to the Men's Club* (Coe 1992), 43% of the women perceived 'the existence of the men's club network as the greatest barrier to women in management.'

One of the difficulties women report is that the sexes can approach the activity differently and, as there are more men in many networks, we have to learn how to operate there. Some refer to networking as a game in which the rules are made by others and are not clear, which does not encourage the sense of being an equal and powerful player. Trying to emulate the approach of another group disadvantages us, as we will never be as good at it as they are.

Some women find that it is easier to network with other women than it is to network with men. In her book *You Just Don't Understand*, Deborah Tannen (1992) reports that women communicate by building rapport, which stems from a desire for affiliation, concern for feelings and the need to be liked by others whereas men communicate by dealing with facts and focus more on status – the 'report' style. This can explain some of the problems we may experience in networking. If we are ambivalent in the first place, any discomfort can lead to our feeling completely negative.

Feelings of discomfort are aroused in some of us at any hint of not being entirely straight with people about the purpose of a relationship. Fear of looking dependent, of appearing a bit pushy or of being in someone's debt are also reasons to reject the activity. Suspicion or assumptions about what people represent can colour our reaction too. In the final analysis, varied demands both in and out of work can leave limited time for what many see as an optional and peripheral activity. We have to consider whether the time investment will be worth it in the long run.

Vicky

'As a senior woman in my organisation I am struck by the difference in attitudes of men and women towards involvement in activities outside their immediate job remit. The men phone me up and ask if there are any interesting projects which they can be considered for. In contrast I have to approach the women and find that it is perceived in terms of will they get extra payment, or where will they find the time. It's as if they do not see the opportunities these different projects will bring them in terms of raising their profile with senior managers and broadening their skills base.'

<u>EXERCISE –</u>
<u>BARRIERS TO NETWORKING</u>

- Write down the negative associations networking has for you and the positive aspects it offers.

THE BENEFITS OF NETWORKING

Apart from building up a range of useful business contacts and expanding our social base, networking can bring a number of other benefits. These include:

- fulfilment of our personal and work goals
- opportunities to help other people achieve their goals

289

- speedier access to useful information, people, products and services that benefit ourselves, our network, our team and our organisation
- useful job and business opportunities
- enhanced exposure and reputation within our particular field

Reputations depend on exposure to others outside our organisation and what people say about us. Headhunters work on what they hear other people say about those they will approach, while much business is conducted on the basis of perceived credibility, competence and positive relationships. If we want to be part of the world

Please take my business card . . . .

of work and contribute powerfully we need to network!

Anna

Anna used networking to help her stay in touch with her workplace while she was on maternity leave. 'I have found that it's very easy to send out powerful signals when going on maternity leave. I could either adopt an attitude of don't get in touch with me – I'm going to "rest and nest", and if I was really ill I would need to do that. The alternative is to educate people about your needs and the fact you would like to remain involved. There is a price to be paid for not staying in touch.

'I have found people will react to whatever I ask of them. When I had my last baby I wrote a list of all the publications, newsletters, briefing notes and memos that I would like to receive. I asked my head of department to phone me once a month to give me the team's brief. I made a point of coming in to help with some interviews, as I thought it was important to have a say on who I would be working with. I kept up with all my friends, who work in different departments, on the phone. When the baby was born I would pop in to see people for lunch and I made a point of attending leaving parties.

'I had learnt from previous experience that if you talk to just one person you get only one viewpoint and that could be quite negative. It's amazing how quickly an organisation moves on if you are out of circulation.'

DEVELOPING OUR APPROACH TO NETWORKING

It is understandable that women who have a lot going on in their lives will be resistant to networking. We have to balance the benefits with the costs and ask ourselves whether we could achieve our personal and work goals more successfully with the help of others. If you have been working in isolation because you were not aware of the value or the ways of networking, the practical tips here may inspire you to action.

Most importantly we need to be clear about the purposes of networking. Confidence in the process is often boosted by making our own rules, setting an agenda of openness and cultivating relationships that are mutually beneficial on our own terms.

---

* *'I believe my effective networking has been with people who are prepared to share information on an equal basis. I have had negative experiences when I've talked openly about my work and the other person has been secretive about theirs. It has felt like a power play.'*

* *'When we set up our network we laid down some ground-rules at the beginning on professional conduct and support. We decided we are there, not only to feather our own nest, but to help others in the process.'*

* *'I believe that there are always enough opportunities to go around. The more you share the more you will receive, but you can operate really well only with like-minded people.'*

The basis of networking is give and take. A willingness to give is a healthy approach; however, some women find this easier than calling in favours and of course this creates imbalance. We do need to be prepared to ask for ourselves. It can be helpful to think of the giving and receiving working within our network as a whole, not always expecting an individual favour back for one made but trusting to the mutual support overall, provided that the relationships are built on trust.

Amelia

Amelia works as an economist for a professional institution. 'I volunteered to attend meetings with representatives from our industry. I make a point of getting there a bit earlier to introduce myself and staying a bit late afterwards to chat with people. I always tell someone if I found something particularly interesting to get the conversation started. Having such a wide range of contacts definitely helped me to get promoted. If I can help any of my contacts I will go out of my way to do it as soon as possible and I have found they do the same thing.'

WHERE TO NETWORK

Although networking can take place anywhere, it useful to practise in an environment with like-minded people who have similar needs or aspirations. A starting point is to join a women's network. These can provide a whole range of benefits depending on the objectives of the network and the women who attend their events. Many of them provide training, social activities, reductions for certain goods and services, newsletters, information and support on career development. Extending and using the women's network balances the power of other networks. This does not mean it is to exclude others.

As the workplace is mixed, we will be limiting

ourselves by just networking with women and we do need to be involved in broadly represen-tative groups.

Anita

'My firm have an appalling track record for training their staff – especially in terms of personal development. I joined my net-work specifically to get the sort of training I knew I could not get at work. As a result of attending the workshops and making a regular commitment to myself to go along – even when I don't really feel like it – I have been promoted. I know the reason why: because I've grown in confidence. I've made a point of applying what I've learnt and I've picked the brains of the other women at the network. People are so flattered to be asked their advice – I learnt to follow it.'

Where we choose to extend our contacts will depend on our interests and objectives. For example we may network through:

- professional associations
- local chambers of commerce
- work-related conferences and events
- training courses
- special interest groups
- sporting groups
- the local church and community activities
- voluntary work

There is a view that if we are really powerfully networking, anyone we want to talk to is only seven people away. Whilst this would be diffi-cult to substantiate, it can be interesting to con-sider whom the people we know network with, and how introductions can be made.

EXERCISE –
NETWORK NET

- On a large sheet of paper draw a diagram of the main groups with which you come into contact, with yourself at the centre.
- Start plotting in the additional contacts you could make.
- Identify how you could instigate the connection.
- Jot down the actions to take.

DOING IT

There is no mystique to networking, however, when attending a formal network event, the following points are useful to bear in mind.

Be clear about what you want

If we are clear about what we want, the process of networking works extremely well. As we get to know people, we need to let them know what we are looking for. It may be that our immediate circle of contacts are exactly the right people, but through sharing our goals and aspirations with them they can signpost us to useful contacts and sources of information.

Approach people first

It is good to make a point of approaching people first. People are often uncomfortable when they do not know anyone, so making the first move breaks the ice. If they are there to network, they will be not only relieved but pleased as well.

Taking the initiative helps us to lead the conversation in directions that interest us.

Give a firm handshake

As we are often judged in the first few seconds of meeting, a firm handshake rather than a 'wet lettuce' gives a more definite impression.

Introduce positively

Once contact has been made, we need to introduce ourself and what we do. We need to describe ourself concisely in a way that differentiates us from others and sounds positive.

Make the conversation two-way

Women are generally known for being great listeners, which is certainly a skill to be valued, and the conversation will be helped if we ask the other person questions about themselves. In a networking situation it is important, however, to make sure they find out about us as well. We should be prepared to feed in personal information, about our experience, relevant skills and knowledge of the particular topic. It is important that we always speak well of ourself and our organisation. We are our own greatest ambassador and people are attracted to success.

Exchange business cards

Giving a business card or exchanging contact details may be appropriate. After the event, writing on the back of the card what we talked about and where we met prevents a meaning-less stack of cards.

Circulate

Moving on can be difficult but preferable to getting stuck with one person when the purpose is to network – or if they are really boring! By using their name, saying we have enjoyed talking, and mentioning the opportunity to meet a lot of people, we can disengage from the conversation.

Maintain contact after the event

ropping a line or phoning important contacts soon after the event maintains the connection. It is very easy for people to forget who they have met at different functions. If the contacts are people we want to meet again, it is important to let the person know why we would like to meet up with them. Be assertive and make a specific date, rather than getting trapped into a vague suggestion of 'we must meet up'.

> ### Nicole
> 'I used to hate the idea of networking. I decided to treat it as a bit of fun rather than a heavy-duty thing I had to do. Once I relaxed and started going to my network regularly and got involved with organising a couple of events I started to reap the benefits. I make a point of finding out what people are interested in and then if I see an article or something which they may not have seen I pop it in the post to them – it's a useful way of them remembering me and it makes it easier to pick their brains when I need help.'

Tell people *how* you need help

If we need help with something specific – such as a project, updating our curriculum vitae, a

297

new job in a different sector – we need to tell people in our network what we are looking for. It may be that the people we meet are not the right people, but they have access to others and can mention us in a conversation with someone who could help. It is up to us to apply this principle too. It is also a courtesy to acknowledge their help and any outcomes of it.

If our contacts pass on someone's name who can help us, the most powerful starting point is to tell the person they have been recognised for their achievements. People love to share their successful experience, whether it is how they managed a project, climbed the career ladder or set up a new business.

Ruth

'When I returned from a two-year break of working abroad I found it very difficult to find work as a copywriter. The recession had really affected my particular field. I decided to work as a freelance writer. The first thing I had to do was phone up anyone and everyone I had ever known in relation to my work – to tell them I was available and to find out where the key people go. I joined a professional association and over a period of time I have build up an impressive range of clients, through using my network of friends and asking if people can suggest who might be interested in what I do.'

Sally

'At a network meeting I met a woman who worked for a company I had always admired. I took the plunge and mentioned it to her. She took my card and said she would see if there was anything going in the department that specialised in my field – graphic design. It was about three weeks later when she said the head of the department might be interested and to send in my curriculum vitae. A few weeks after that they asked to see *my portfolio and I went for an interview. I'm now working for the company of my dreams.'*

The four essential ingredients for effective networking are:

- a positive attitude – the most effective net-workers enjoy the process
- reciprocity – this involves supporting others without expecting anything in return, and asking for help too
- a strategic approach – we need to be careful in our selection of networks, groups or organisations, have good knowledge of our contacts and make clear requests when we ask for help
- time investment – we benefit from joining a formal network only if we go to meetings; keeping in touch builds up emotional currency

<u>EXERCISE –
NETWORK PLAN</u>

- Join a network and go to meetings or revive your existing contacts.
- Once you are clear about your career or personal development goals, identify the people who might be able to help you.
- Draw up a plan of action to contact them.

BUILDING RELATIONSHIPS WITHIN THE ORGANISATION

If the quality of our working life is dependent on our relationships we need to think about how

we can enhance the quality of those relationships – with those above us, with those at our
own level and with those below us in the organisation's hierarchy.

MANAGING YOUR MANAGER

Although conditioning may have taught us to
accept authority, it is essential to break that
pattern and make the conscious decision to collaborate with the person we are immediately
responsible to as an equal person. Adopting this
approach can make a difference to our:

- self-confidence
- career development
- motivation
- stress levels
- ability to get the job done
- general working environment

Many of us may be inclined to put the onus of
responsibility for maintaining the quality of this
relationship on the manager rather than on our
own shoulders. This approach is increasingly
being seen as outmoded as organisations
develop flatter structures that require effective
teamwork across functions.

It is a relationship of mutual dependence.
John Gabarro and John Kotter (1993) of the
Harvard Business School suggest that 'managing your boss means the process of consciously
working with your superior to obtain the best
possible results for you, your boss and your
company'. The principle of making the most of
our team's strengths and getting help from them
to balance out our weaknesses also applies to

our working relationship with our own manager. We need to understand the boss's organisational and personal goals, expectations, pressures and workstyle and the context in which they operate.

How we view our manager

If we want to build an effective relationship with our managers we need to think about the information we have about them and its sources, what has created our current view and how we can extend that view.

If we or our manager are new to the role we will not have a great deal to go on. It is important not to base our current relationship on the previous relationship with our last boss, but instead to make a fresh start.

It may be that we have worked with our manager for so long that we have begun to lose sight of what makes them tick, have stopped reading the situation afresh and are working on assumptions or hearsay. Previous experience may have distorted our view or it may have been coloured inappropriately by particularly negative or positive team members. The prejudices of others can get in the way of a potentially good relationship. Managing the manager involves striving to develop our own working relationship based on accurate information and a positive approach.

Information sources

Questioning what we do know about the manager forces attention on where we get the information and whether we are taking it all at face value. Do we have accurate knowledge or are we working on assumptions? If the latter, can we test the assumptions? Do others' perceptions and anecdotes reinforce or challenge our views?

If we are unsure about what makes our manager tick, we need to find out more. Apart from the obvious method of asking them directly, we can approach the situation more subtly in conversation and by observation and interaction at:

- one-to-one meetings
- team meetings
- conferences
- the organisation's social activities

Further information can be gathered by noting:

- what they attend or get involved with
- their interactions with close colleagues
- which newspapers and journals they read
- what committees and working parties they attend
- their interests

We can also ask others for their observations and check them against our own impressions.

Our manager's agenda

Our role is to help the organisation fulfil its objectives, and these determine our manager's objectives. Is his or her main purpose to:

* increase profits?

- reduce costs?
- improve efficiency?
- raise the profile of the organisation?
- develop new products or services?
- something else?

Our understanding of our boss's agenda and the context in which they operate is helped if we have a sense of why they were appointed to the job and how their background and experience are relevant. If we appreciate their key objectives and focus for the organisation, we will see the reasoning behind certain decisions, and appreciate what sort of information will be helpful to them and how best to present our ideas and slant specific projects or requests. It is also worth thinking about the agenda of their own boss.

Olive
Olive works as the Head of Information in a professional association. 'Our new Director General wants to raise the profile of the association within the industry. I have made a point of joining various working parties and have recognised that my department can fulfil a really useful role in publishing reports – this is a new initiative for our area.'

Catherine
Catherine works in a public relations consultancy. 'I always have to think through how to approach my boss for certain resources for a campaign. If I say to her, "This will generate this sort of coverage for the client", she tends not to be so enthusiastic as when I say "If we use this approach, we can save a large proportion of costs for the firm if we run this campaign". Then she really will sit and listen. I've learnt from experience. Her concern is not just doing a good job, but also the effect

it will have on the company. I was not used to this at first, but it really makes me think about my overall approach for getting her support.'

EXERCISE –
SEEK TO UNDERSTAND YOUR MANAGER

- Research your manager. In particular identify their job focus, main organisational issues and key objectives.
- With this knowledge, plan your best approach.

Values and personal goals

Apart from organisational goals most of us have personal goals related to work and career. If we want to be successful we need to bear this in mind when we approach our managers for help and resources – in other words: what's in it for them?

Personal aspirations are usually more difficult to establish than organisational objectives. However, if we have a sufficiently good relationship with our manager it may be worth taking the risk and discussing such topics openly. Observing their behaviour and what they talk about is another approach.

Our boss's career ambitions can be indicated by the way they focus their energies.

- What do we know about our boss's interests and what they value?
- What are their particular circumstances?
- Do they like to work late or balance their home and work life?

- How do they spend their leisure time?
- Do they spend more time on the impression they are giving to their seniors or are they more concerned with the performance of members of their team?
- Do they particularly enjoy raising their profile outside the organisation or are they happy for members of the team to take on that function because they have no particular desire for the limelight?
- What is their attitude to personal and professional development for themselves and other members of staff?
- What is their attitude to women in the team and the organisation?

Lorraine

Lorraine works for a trade union and had recently started a job with a new manager in the Information Department. 'At first I could not understand why my manager was so off-hand with me every time I came back from giving a presentation to other heads of department or senior managers, until a colleague pointed out to me I was stealing his limelight. She said that our role was to prepare the information for him when requests came in – not to deliver it as well. I am not used to this as in my last job my boss was only too happy for me to get on with it. His behaviour is really making me think about whether I want to stay.'

EXERCISE – WHAT DRIVES YOUR MANAGER?

Try to ascertain your manager's values and personal motivations.
- How do these compare or contrast with your own?

Their pressures

Understanding the pressures our managers are under and what we can do to alleviate them will make a difference to our relationship with them. The pressures can come from a variety of sources, such as their own boss, the team, their colleagues or outside the organisation. Being sensitive to them and minimising the amount of stress we create for them will have an impact on how they perceive us.

This does not mean that we should hide information or problems from our managers, but it does require us to think through how we can project a positive image and look for solutions rather than problems when we spend time with them. We may not have thought through the exact solution our manager would subscribe to; however, having a go not only demonstrates initiative, but also saves our manager's time. No manager has the monopoly on good ideas, so doing as much as we can to help the situation along will probably be much appreciated.

Strengths and weaknesses

Just as we need to be aware of our own strengths and weaknesses, so appreciation of those of our manager is essential. By acknowledging and working to our managers' strengths and redressing their weaknesses not only will we be appreciated by our managers, but we could also develop useful development and career opportunities.

Jemima

'I don't know how my last boss got to his current position without understanding budgets and finance but he had a real aversion to figures and anything that required detailed thought. At first it was not my strength but I realised that someone in the team had to deal with it, so I offered to take it on soon after he was appointed. He was really grateful and arranged for me to have lots of training on spreadsheets and finance itself. My role was to keep him regularly informed and he would take me into meetings because of my detailed knowledge. As a result I became known to other senior managers and was well placed when a promotion opportunity arose. I am now training up one of my team, but I have good grasp of the situation as well.'

Yvette
'My boss used to organise our industry's largest exhibition in this country. He used to hate it because it involved a lot of detail and large-scale presentations. He used to involve me with some of it. Over a period of time he has delegated more and more, until one day I asked him outright if I could do the whole thing. He was over the moon.'

Michelle
'My director is supposed to be responsible for the annual sales conference. For the past few years it hasn't gone very well because he never sees anything through to the end. He has also lost enthusiasm for the whole enterprise. I offered to take it over. It's been incredibly useful because I organise the seating plans for the formal dinner. I have to talk to all the senior managers in the company and find out what they are doing. It's not only raised my profile, but it has also helped me understand the company in the broadest sense.'

A regular working relationship

Understanding the changing dynamics of our relationship with the manager can help us manage our reactions. Observing their reactions in different circumstances will reveal useful information to help us maximise the working relationship. In addition to our own experience, how do they work with different people and what seems to delight or frustrate them?

Lilian

Lilian had transferred from one department where she had started as a trainee to another department, where she was now a professional accountant. 'When I first started with my current boss I really irritated her because I behaved in the manner my former boss had responded to. I would become the little girl and flatter him and really appreciate everything he did for me. My current boss told me that she did not need to be flattered and that if I had a problem to come straight out with it rather than giving her a big build-up of how great she was. It seems ridiculous now because my current boss treats me like an intelligent adult; however it was the behaviour that worked for me in my former situation.'

Working preferences and communication styles

To find out how the boss likes to work, we can identify if their preferences are for:

- variety or routine
- broad brush or detail
- taking risks or playing safe
- working with people or systems
- procedures or results
- 'reading' or 'listening'
- frequent communication or managing at a distance

Preferences for communication styles can create unease if they conflict with our expectations or preferences. For example, does the manager prefer broad-ranging discussion or a tight and structured agenda? If we have a new manager it is worth establishing fairly quickly how they want to work with us by asking directly and by spending some time reviewing the working process jointly.

Peter Drucker divides managers into 'listeners' and 'readers' (cited in Gabarro & Kotter 1993) . The 'listener' boss likes to receive information in person and ask questions. 'Reader' bosses like detailed reports to study before the meeting. A 'reader' manager may well perceive us as unprofessional for not being prepared if we are used to working with a 'listener'. A manager who is a 'listener' when we are used to a 'reader' could be irritated by the amount of detail we give them.

It may be that their style of working is not compatible with our own. If we have a 'reader' boss and our style is that of 'listener' we can help the relationship by, for example, sending a detailed memo in advance of the meeting covering the key points. The meeting can then be used to clarify and discuss any further points. This will speed up the approval process and satisfy both parties more. This preference will also apply to the way they present information.

If we have a boss who wants a low level of involvement with their staff and we require a fairly high level of guidance, we will need to make more of an effort in developing our support network at work. In these situations it is helpful to reflect on each others' strengths and weaknesses to identify very specifically where the boss can provide us with help. If the boss is too busy to help us we will need to be assertive and ask them who else we could go to for support.

Every time we meet with our manager we need to think through exactly what we want to discuss with them. It may be worth sending a brief agenda in advance so there are no surprises for them. One-to-one meetings are essentially for reviewing our work since we last met up with them, particularly in terms of informing them of our achievements, and for clarifying the next stage in our workload. This is also the time to discuss any problems and put forward possible solutions.

As a higher premium than ever before is being placed on teamwork, one way of demonstrating this is by not only telling our manager when we have worked well with other people, but also having the generosity of spirit to flag up our colleagues' achievements.

If we disagree with our manager's line of approach, the meeting is the time to say so. Disagreement can be positive if we give alternatives and our reasons.

EXERCISE – COMMUNICATION FREQUENCY AND WORKING PREFERENCES

- Analyse your manager's communication style and your own.
- How would you describe your boss's working preferences – and your own?
- How can you manage any differences?
- See how you can modify your working relationship by small changes to reach solutions more effectively.

Many of us – including those more senior – do not get enough praise. If we genuinely think our manager has been helpful or done something well, it is worth giving them positive feedback on the results and impact of their actions. If we do not feel we are getting sufficient feedback on our performance, in terms of either the things our manager believes we have done well or the areas in which we need to improve, the one-to-one meeting is the place to raise the issue. It is wise to adhere to the principle of supporting people in public and disagreeing with them in private.

There may come a point when we find our boss's behaviour is unacceptable.

---

*   *'My manager was spending so much time playing politics and not getting on with the job that it was ridiculous.'*
*   *'I found that every time I had to involve my boss in any activity it took twice as long.'*
*   *'I had to cover up for her incompetence all the time.'*
*   *'I felt that my manager was a bully and was out to get at me.'*

In a situation that has become intolerable, despite assertive communication and after exploration of every option, it may be that the time has come for us to transfer or leave.

WORKING WITH COLLEAGUES

Many women report that they develop personal relationships because they like the person rather than for professional reasons, yet a range of relationships and contacts will broaden our understanding. Moreover, good relationships with our peers enable us to cut through red tape and mobilise support for the issues that really matter, enhance our knowledge of the potential opportunities and ultimately help us to fulfil our organisational objectives. Our peers are not just the people at the same level as us, they could be more senior or more junior – their status is irrelevant to getting the job done.

Carol
'I have found the most useful thing I can do is to listen to what my colleagues have to say in terms of their experience and knowledge. By really valuing what they do and trying to understand what they are trying to achieve I have found we can help each other. In the past I used to think, "well of course you would think that, you are an accountant", but by changing my approach I can see how we can collaborate together. It has taught me to think more laterally.'

Peer support and effective teamwork go hand in hand. In our current highly competitive climate, organisations need teams of people to work together rather than be drawn into internal fighting. As we move on professionally it is likely we will be part of management teams needing to work cross-functionally, and if we are more familiar with the disciplines of managing down it can be hard to change our approach. In any group of people, different needs will prevail:

- individuals will have their own agendas, foibles and issues
- there will be tasks to tackle that drive the activity
- the working process of the team or the relationship will demand attention

Healthy and productive relationships grow if we balance these three elements. This means:

- Appreciating and supporting colleagues in the achievement of their personal objectives or goals – as far as is compatible with our personal integrity
- Ensuring that we work together effectively to achieve team and thus organisational goals
- Tackling   difficulties   and   addressing problems

Recognising our mutual interdependence is the first step towards professional relationships that benefit both parties.

Enhancing our relationships with colleagues

It is rare that we work in isolation. We need to be aware of the colleagues outside our immediate team who are essential to our effectiveness at work.

> ## EXERCISE –
> ## ESSENTIAL COLLEAGUES
>
> - Make a list of the colleagues outside your immediate team with whom you come into contact in doing your job.
> - For each one, rate the quality of the present relationship and plan how you can develop it further.

Managing relationships with our colleagues across the organisation generally is as essential – and as difficult – as managing up, and requires that we apply the same principles:

- gather information
- think about the other person's position and try to see things from their point of view
- communicate assertively
- value difference and work effectively together to accommodate it
- review performance regularly

Regular communication is essential to sustain relationships, not just within the day-to-day business context but also informally through occasional lunches, drinks after work or by joining in the organisation's social activities.

Georgia

'I was conscious that the people who seemed to know what was going on were the staff and managers who went to this particular wine bar at lunchtime. Our managing director holds court there for all the other senior managers. If you go there he

invariably sends over a bottle of wine and eventually you are invited to join him at his table. I would go along with some colleagues. It seemed a bit pretentious at first, but it's a great way of getting to know people. I noticed when I stopped going for a while that I was completely out of date with what was going on with the company.'

The type of support we offer our colleagues can include keeping their confidence, speaking well of them to other people in the organisation or acting as a sounding board over particular problems. Actively listening to our peers, by putting aside our own personal agenda and valuing their right to their own opinions and values, is the highest compliment we can pay them. Acting with integrity and honesty is essential if we are to maintain good relationships.

Team working

A prerequisite for team working is being clear about where we are going. If the team is cross-functional, the objectives can get muddled or distorted by the focus of different departments. Defining and agreeing the team direction is an excellent procedure in every team meeting.

If we are working collaboratively it is essential to develop an accurate picture of the strengths and weaknesses of other team members. Similarly, being honest about our own limitations and capabilities will indicate our integrity and professionalism to our colleagues. Although taking risks is important for our personal development, when we are working on an important project with a team we need to play to our

315

strengths, rather than use it as an opportunity to develop the areas in which we need to improve.

EXERCISE –
TEAM STRENGTHS

- When working in a team answer the following questions:
  What is this team trying to achieve?
  What skills and strengths do we have that will help us achieve? How can we make greater use of them?
  Where does each person's role fit in?
  How can each person's goals(s) be met?

Dealing with difficulties

Conflict can arise if we do not keep the channels of communication open between us and our peers. During times of change or altered circumstances it is easy to neglect communication or resort to the written word, yet it is precisely at such times that we need to keep talking to avoid a distortion of the facts.

However, it can be vital at times of upheaval to choose with whom and about what we communicate. Rivalry can intrude in relationships with colleagues, obscuring communication, undermining effective team working and threatening results. Problems can arise when personal position is threatened or potential loss of power is perceived. Organisational change creates insecurity and will witness greater activity in the political tactics arena.

Some people act like this as a matter of routine and some organisations are characterised by regular high-level political activity. We need to be sensitive to what is going on and recognise that people are not always genuine and sincere. Of course, the very nature of such behaviour means that it is hard to pinpoint. However, if we are ever confused by outcomes or feel that there are things going on that are not as they seem, it is likely that political tactics are operating.

Tactics to be alert to are:

- **information control** – from concealing, withholding or filtering information to telling lies; selectively consulting and taking advice from certain quarters only; maintaining a broad informal network
- **forming mutually beneficial alliances** – to plot a course of action, to get a decision through, to manoeuvre an outcome, to oust or instate a colleague
- **maintaining options** – not committing to a particular course of action, saying one thing and doing another, making public statements that are negated in practice, witholding complete support until essential

  It may be expedient to act in similar ways, although we believe that we should act in ways that we can justify within our value system. By observing, listening, thinking clearly about desired outcomes and planning the best means to achieve them, we can extend our choices and often our power.

317

EXERCISE –
TACTICS

- Think of a difficult situation at work that you are or have been involved in. Ask yourself:
  Who were the main parties and what were they trying to achieve?
  What tactics do you think others were deploying?
  What tactics would you be prepared to use yourself.

---

* *'When I am putting forward a proposition for a new company initiative to senior management, I have learnt always to ring around a few key contacts to gauge their reaction and build up their support before the crucial meeting.'*

* *'I learnt from bitter experience that if I was chairing a difficult meeting it is more effective to hold it in my office. When I had held awkward meetings at other people's premises they could stage manage events to the extent that it sabotaged the progress of the meeting and its purpose.'*

* *'I have become aware that my organisation is incredibly political and I am uncomfortable with this. However, I have learnt to be more observant of the interactions, more attuned to what is going on that is not always obvious and to*

> *   *think more strategically about my objec-
> tives for the department and how to
> achieve them.'*

Specific problems may necessitate confronting someone about the effect of actions on us.
Although this may be difficult, the assertive
framework as explored in Chapters 5 and 6
gives us the basis for action. By focusing on the
issue or the behaviour rather than criticising
the person, the result will be less damaging long
term.

Laura

*'I work with a male colleague who is not a very good listener. He
is brilliant at selling in certain circumstances, but if the client
does not get enthused or has problems, he literally switches off.
I usually end up rescuing the situation. I have confronted him
on one occasion and he was a bit resistant to what I was saying, but finally he conceded that he does get bored.*

*'Recently we were in a meeting with a client and my col-
league was getting irritated. He was really quite offhand to the
client. I couldn't believe what he was doing. When we came out
of the meeting I had to go on to another meeting somewhere
else. I haven't spoken to him about it because I've been so
angry and we haven't had any privacy. As a result I find myself
avoiding contact with him. We will be working together again so
I do need to tell him how I feel, otherwise it's going to get in the
way of our work.'*

In certain situations we need to weigh up how
important an issue is for us before we confront a
peer. If it is a matter of principle, we need to
decide whether we need to lose the battle in
order to win the war. We should also be wary of-

imposing our point of view as the correct one. Always scoring points and never admitting to making mistakes will alienate us from our peers. A more effective process would be to talk through the reasons why we would adopt a certain stance and the consequences of any decisions taken for a particular issue. It may be that we have to agree to disagree.

INFLUENCING AND BEING INFLUENCED

Influencing involves attempting to modify or change someone else's attitudes and/or behaviour and it happens frequently in relationships. There are many ways – both overt and covert – in which we influence or are influenced. These can be analysed and grouped in categories. Our influencing style is defined according to the sense or personal needs to which we predominantly appeal as we communicate.

- **head** – presenting a logical argument supported by facts, information and figures appealing to the intellect
- **pressure** – offering inducement or threatening sanctions, appealing to senses of duty, fear, responsibility, concern for security or desire for reward
- **emotion** – creating enthusiasm for possibilities and vision of the future, generating shared belief and commitment
- **affiliation** – gaining commitment through a desire for personal association, connection with or approval from another and/or a relationship based on admiration or responding to personal charisma

> * *I believe we should relocate. The figures have proven that it is getting more and more expensive to run this office. If we moved out of the city we would have much lower overheads and we would have better access to the airport for seeing clients in Europe.*
>
> * *If we don't sort this problem out, the Health and Safety Executive will have us in court for being negligent. It's that serious.*
>
> * *As an organisation we have made a difference to 2,000 homeless people this year. I want us to continue with this impressive track record; however we have to work even harder at the fundraising and cut costs.*
>
> * *I want you all to know I've really valued your support through this difficult time. I believe all of you have worked incredibly hard and I am impressed by your commitment. We need to build on that commitment as we tackle this new project.*

To be effective, we need to appreciate our own and others' preferences and develop our capacity to employ different styles according to:

- the person we are trying to influence, their position and preferred style
- the environment and context
- our preferred style, our communication

skills, our self-awareness and self-esteem, and our energy levels

- the particular issue

It is important to decide what we want to achieve, to focus on outcomes and plan how we will do so, to take advantage of opportunities that arise and to allow ourselves thinking time. Approaching individuals to put our case rather than taking on the whole group collectively will help if we are in a minority. Sounding out our colleagues' support before we get to a critical decision-making time smooths the process.

MANAGING A TEAM

The greatest challenge for any manager is to harness the talent, creativity and skills of their team for the good of the organisation, the community, the team and the individual. Our staff are critical to the achievement and fulfilment of our objectives. If they succeed we can enjoy their glory; if they fail we are accountable for their inability to deliver.

Good management practice in essence is about empowering others, a natural part of empowering ourself. Treating others as we would wish to be treated involves sharing power and not pulling any ladder up behind us. It arises from an open agenda, a belief in the potential of people and a desire to help others as well as ourselves grow to reach our potential.

There is a whole range of publications and courses by the Industrial Society on managing and empowering people, which will enable us to get the best out of our staff.

Recent research in the United States suggests

that regular meetings between a manager and each team member had a positive effect on all aspects of the organisation's quality, morale and productivity. On average, a minimum of one meeting a month should be scheduled in each person's diary. However, this will depend on the nature of the work.

Managers and their teams on Industrial Society courses report the following benefits of regular meetings:

- time is saved in the long term because the team member does not have to keep popping in to see the manager.
- there is a general improvement in the quality of the relationship because both parties have a deeper understanding of what motivates and frustrates them
- conflict situations are nipped in the bud before they get blown out of proportion
- the annual appraisal or performance review is more focused on looking forward rather than dwelling on the past because problems have been addressed throughout the year – and there are no surprises for either party.
- regular communication ensures both parties are well informed as situations arise

The level of day-to-day involvement and the quality of the time we spend with our team will determine the level of trust developed and can minimise conflict.

In order to empower others and build a power-ful relationship with staff, managers can follow certain principles:

323

- treat people with respect and dignity
- ensure staff are clear about their objectives and have the resources to carry out their work
- set clear guidelines on acceptable standards and behaviour
- give regular feedback
- regularly communicate with staff
- listen to their ideas in one-to-one and team meetings
- give credit for their ideas and actions in public to members of the team and other managers
- create an environment of continuous learning, through training, coaching and personal development
- allow people to make mistakes and learn from them
- address problems before they become crises
- delegate interesting projects to enable others to grow, not only giving out the tasks you do not enjoy.
- praise and support in public and discipline in private.
- act with integrity by carrying out agreed actions or explaining why things have not been done
- genuinely consult the team on decisions and actions
- train up your successor
- give people as much control and responsibility for their work as possible
- make the customer the focus of the team's reason to exist
- explain the reasons and impact of change

- enable and value people's solutions to problems
- value different approaches, perspectives, opinions and experience
- focus on what the individual can do rather than dwelling on their weaknesses
- value and recognise teamwork
- attend management courses regularly to keep up to date
- share power with the team

Susie

'I have a really good team of people. It has taken time to build them up but it is probably the most worthwhile thing I have ever done. People often do not see their own gifts and talents. I think part of the role of a manager is to create an environment where people can flourish.'

OTHER IMPORTANT RELATIONSHIPS

It is empowering to treat everyone with the same courtesy, whatever their position in the organisation. People who are more senior than us can have a significant impact, not only on our effectiveness in the job but also on our career progress. We can benefit by personal encouragement in addition to credibility as a result of our associations. Relationships with secretarial staff will also be important.

Secretaries

Positive relationships have to be worked on and have to work both ways. Thinking of the other person and their work situation can reveal ways that we can be helpful. As most administrative

325

staff are women, this is where we can have impact on the culture of the organisation.

Many women on our courses report that getting access to the management grapevine is extremely difficult if they are in a minority. One way of overcoming this is by building up a good relationship of mutual support with the secretaries of senior managers. An effective secretary will be the manager of the manager's time and will know their movements, the activities in which they are involved, the people with whom the manager is regularly in contact and the issues they consider important.

The secretary can, in effect, act as our sponsor by putting forward our name when the manager is looking to involve people. As with all relationships, this one can be reciprocal if we also provide support.

> * *'In our company the informal network is the 'men only' boxing dinners. My greatest source of information are the secretaries of the managers – without them my job would be impossible.'*
>
> * *'Before I had children I didn't mind going drinking with the guys, but now it is out of the question. The secretaries are wonderful allies and they really do know what's going on.'*
>
> * *'I always make an effort to have a chat with our secretaries. Apart from the fact I really like them, they act as my sponsors because they put my name forward to their managers for any interesting projects.'*

> *   '*I was having real difficulties with a pro-
> ject and needed information fast from a
> senior manager. I've always had a good
> relationsip with his secretary. She made
> me an appointment for the next day;
> usually it takes two weeks.*'

Mentors

In organisations where women are under-
represented or if we have ambitious career
aspirations a mentor can help us in several
areas. These include:

- helping us recognise and develop career
  opportunities
- providing feedback on our performance and
  how we are perceived
- identifying who the key players are within
  the organisation
- advising us how to conduct ourselves in
  meetings and organisational gatherings
- advising us on training and skills that we will
  need for the future
- introducing us to important people for our
  career development
- explaining how power is exercised in the
  organisation

Some organisations provide a formal mentoring scheme, in which case we can ask to participate. If there is no such scheme, it is a case of
deciding whether someone inside or outside our
organisation would be more appropriate. Our
mentor does not have to be very senior within

327

the organisation but must have a genuine commitment developing people and must be prepared to spend time with us on a regular basis.

Megan

'I was promoted into an all-male department. To be frank with you, virtually all of them were real chauvinists, including the head of department. He felt quite uncomfortable with me, so he decided to appoint one of his most experienced team members as my mentor. This chap was also very traditional in his views, but underpinning all his prejudices was real belief in the development of people.

'He gave me a lot of guidance and he defended me against the other men. I think he really enjoyed helping me. I am really grateful to him for starting me on the road of my professional career.'

If we are clear about where we are now and where we want to get to, it is easier to identify the best person to enable us to fulfil our goals. Criteria will include:

- their experience, skills, strengths, weaknesses and position
- how they are viewed within and outside the organisation
- what sort of people they have influence with

It is vital to choose someone we can trust, who is honest and a good communicator and listener, and also someone who can enthuse and motivate people.

Liza

'When I joined my organisation, about two-thirds of the staff had been made redundant. There was noone senior to manage

me, so I was put in with an unrelated department. The head of department was not at all interested in my function and he seemed to take an instant dislike to me. I tried extremely hard to get on with him, but I could see he viewed me as an inconvenience.

'*In the end I went to see a senior manager who had always expressed some interest in my area. He could not see a practical way of taking me on as a direct report, so I asked him if he would be my mentor. At the time I did not realise how senior he was. It was agreed that I would report to my current manager for the day-to-day operational work, but I would see my mentor for the overall strategic issues.*

'*He has given me extremely useful feedback on how to promote my area, improve my performance and sort out difficult problems. He is very decisive, trustworthy and focused about what needs to be done. He has helped me overcome certain problems I have had as woman in a predominantly male environment.*'

An external mentor can bring a different set of benefits and disadvantages. They are not personally involved in the organisation and will not have any particular axe to grind. They can give us a fresh perspective when looking at a particular problem. Some may have useful external contacts and can give us some insight into how our organisation is viewed from outside. The main disadvantage is that they will not have a very full picture, so they can give us only personal reactions to what we tell them.

When establishing the relationship with a mentor it is worth setting down some clear guidelines on the frequencey of meetings and the areas in which we would welcome their input. They are there not to fix us or solve our problems but to enable us to think more clearly about how we tackle the issues we have agreed to work on.

It is important to evaluate progress with the relationship from time to time. It may take a few meetings before an easy rapport is developed. If the relationship has fulfilled its original objective, it could be worth assessing the value of continuing on another goal or ending the mentoring relationship.

Isabel

'My mentor was a speaker at my local women's network. I went up and complimented on her excellent speech. It was really helpful for me at the time. I identified with the sorts of problems she had experienced and admired her positive approach to life generally. I asked her outright if she would be my mentor.

'It is really useful to talk to someone who is very senior and who is totally unconnected to what I do. However, people's problems seem to be the same the world over. She is really encouraging and challenging and has forced me to think about what I want to do in the long term. She has the most amazing array of contacts. I noticed that she wrote to me within a week of meeting me, so she has taught me how to maintain contact after meeting with someone. It's so easy to take a business card and just forget the whole thing.

'It's fascinating being with someone whose only motive is altruistic. She has this gift of developing people. She met her secretary in a shop and trained her up to be a really top P.A. It's made me realise that if she can do this for others, one day I can do it for someone else.'

Sponsors

Sponsors are managers who are more senior than us in the organisational hierarchy. They can benefit us in a number of ways including:

- speaking up for us to become involved in interesting projects because they are aware of our capabilities
- backing us in times of conflict, which gives us credibility that we would not normally have without their patronage
- introducing us to useful contacts and passing on pertinent information to which we would not normally have access

The relationship with a sponsor is not necessarily developed through approaching them for support, as we could do with a mentor. The system generally works through us raising our visibility by the activities in which we become involved, as indicated in Chapter 7.

EXERCISE – ADDITIONAL RELATIONSHIPS

- Think about any additional relationships that would help you to be effective at work and in your career.
- If you need a sponsor or mentor, identify suitable people and consider the most effective approach.
- Become a mentor or sponsor.

Kathleen

'I changed my position from being a personnel officer to a human resource executive. My new role is more of a facilitation and advisory position to very senior managers who want added value in dealing with people. I had to visit them to introduce myself and what I could do for them, based on what I had achieved for other people. It took time for me to build up my confidence. I asked the senior managers who had been pleased

with my approach and the results and owed me some favours
if they would endorse me with their peer group. They were only
too happy to help.'

SUMMARY –
PRACTICAL TIPS

* Clarify your objectives for networking
* Identify ways you can help people in your network
* Approach people first at a networking event
* Check out your manager's personal and professional objectives
* Find out more about your manager
* Offer to take on tasks your manager does not enjoy
* Tell your colleagues how good they are
* Tell your boss what you value about your colleagues
* Build powerful relationships with your peers
* Empower your people
* Get to know the secretaries and administrators in your workplace
* Ask someone to be your mentor
* Mentor someone else

BIBLIOGRAPHY

ACAS (1987) *Discipline at Work. The ACAS Advisory Handbook*, Advisory, Conciliation and Arbitration Service.

Back, Ken, and Back, Kate (1992) *Assertiveness at Work – A practical guide to handling awkward situations*, McGraw-Hill.

Baddeley, Simon, and James, Kim (1987) 'Owl, Fox, Donkey or Sheep: Political skills for managers', *Management Education and Development*, vol.18.

Clance, Pauline Rose, and O'Toole, Maureen Ann (1988) 'The Imposter Phenomen: An internal barrier to empowerment and achievement', in Esther D. Rothblum and Ellen Cole, *Treating Women's Fear of Failure*, The Haworth Press.

Coe, Trudy (1992) *The Key to the Men's Club*, The Institute of Management.

Davidson, Marilyn (1985) *Reach for the Top*, Piatkus.

EOC (1993) *Women and Men in Britain 1993*, Equal Opportunities Commission, September.

Forrest, Andrew, and Tolfree, Patrick (1992) *Leaders. The Learning Curve of Achievement.* The Industrial Society.

Gabarro, John J., and Kotter, John P. (1993) 'Managing Your Boss', *Harvard Business Review*, May–June.

Gallie, Duncan, and White, Michael (1993) *Employee Commitment and the Skills Revolution*, PSI Publishing.

Hall, Eric, and Hall, Carol (1988) *Human Relations in Education*, Routledge.

Handy, Charles (1989) *The Age of Unreason*, Century Hutchinson.

Handy, Charles (1984) *The Future of Work*, Basil Blackwell.

Handy, Charles (1985) *Understanding Organisations*, Penguin Business Library.

Hathway, Patti, and Schubert, Susan (1992) *Managing Your Boss*, Kogan Page.

InterExec (1993) *InterExec Client Placement Survey*, June.

Josefowitz, Natasha (1983) *Is This Where I Was Going?* Columbus Books.

Kanter, Rosabeth Moss (1979) *Men and Women of the Corporation*, Basic Books.

Kolb, David A., Rubin, Irwin M. and McIntyre, James M. (1974) *Organisational Psychology: An Experiential Approach to Organisational Behaviour,*Prentice Hall.

La Rouche, Janice, and Ryan, Regina (1988) *Working Women – Strategies for Survival and Success*, Unwin Paperbacks.

McKenna, Douglas D., and McHenry, Jeffrey J.P. (1994) *Positive Politics at Work*, Business One Irwin.

Men 2000 (1994) London: Mintel.

Millman, Val (1985) 'Breadwinning and Babies. A Redefinition of Careers Education', in G. Weiner (ed.), *Just a Bunch of Girls*, Open University Press.

Rowntree, Derek (1991) *How to Manage Your Boss*, Sphere Books.

Ryan, Margaret (ed.) (1986) *Power and Influence in Organisations*, Manpower Services Commission.

Segerman-Peck, Lily M. (1991) *Network and Monitoring. A Women's Guide*, Piatkus.

Shaevitz, Marjorie (1984) *The Superwomen Syndrome*, Fontana/Collins.

Stanford, Janis, and Gardiner, Jo (1993) *No Offence? Sexual Harassment, How It Happens and How to Beat It. A Good Practice Guide and Survey Results*, The Industrial Society.

Tannen, Deborah (1992) *You Just Don't Understand. Women and Men in Conversation*, Virago.

White, Peter (1981) *Preparing for the Top*, The Industrial Society.

Willis, Liz, and Daisley, Jenny (1990) *Springboard Women's Development Workbook*, Hawthorn Press.

FURTHER READING

For those interested in reading further, we have found the following books useful, arranged under chapter topics.

GENERAL

Paths to Power, Natasha Josefowitz, Columbus Books, 1980

Feminity, Susan Brownmiller, Paladin, 1986

Women and Power, Rosalind Miles, Futura, 1985

The Road Less Travelled, Scott Peck, Arrow, 1990

CAREER AND LIFE PLANNING

Managing Personal Change, Cynthia Scott and Dennis Joffe, Kogan Page, 1992.

Marketing Yourself, Dorothy Leeds, Piatkus, 1991

The Perfect CV, Max Eggert, Century Business, 1992

The Career Discovery Project, Gerald M. Sturman, Aurum Press, 1993

STRESS

Perfect Time Management, Ted Johns, Century Business, 1993

The Stress Work Book. How individuals, teams and organisations can balance pressure and performance, Eve Warren and Caroline Toll, Nicholas Brealey, 1993

SELF-ESTEEM

Feel the Fear and Do It Anyway, Susan Jeffers, Arrow, 1987

Revolution for Within. A Book of Self-Esteem, Gloria Steinem, Bloomsbury, 1992

The Woman's Book of Confidence, Sue Patton Thoele, Conari Press, 1992

Women and Self-Esteem. Understanding the Way We Think and Feel about Ourselves, Linda Tschirhart Sanford and Mary Ellen Donovan, Penguin Books, 1985

ASSERTIVENESS

A Woman in Your Own Right, Anne Dickson, Quartet, 1982

Positive Management, Paddy O'Brien, Nicholas Brealey, 1992

ORGANISATIONAL POWER, POLITICS AND RELATIONSHIPS

Power Networking. 55 Secrets for Personal and Professional Success, Donna and Sandy Vilas, Mountain Harbour Publications, 1991

Corporate Cultures – The Rights and Rituals of Corporate Life, Terence Deal and Allen Kennedy, Penguin Business, 1988